TRUTH
OF
THE STOCK TAPE

A STUDY OF THE STOCK AND COMMODITY MARKETS

WITH CHARTS AND RULES FOR SUCCESSFUL

TRADING AND INVESTING

By

William D. Gann

———————

A practical book written by a successful Wall Street man who has proved his theory in actual trading. He writes from twenty years' experience and gives examples of his rules by the Case System.

This is the only book published covering the investment and speculative field of Cotton and Grain as well as Stocks. It is fully illustrated with 22 charts showing plainly the successful method of trading.

In four books under one cover:

Cover Design: J.Neuman

PREFACE

"Receive my instruction, and not silver; and knowledge rather than choice gold. For wisdom is better than rubies, and all the things that may be desired are not to be compared to it."-- PROV. 8: 10-11.

In addressing you on the subject of investing your surplus funds, I might state that there is no other subject which I could select that so closely concerns your welfare and regarding which you might receive valuable assistance from my instructions.

In the United States a stupendous sum, reaching into millions of dollars, is wasted annually in foolish speculations and unwise investments. This senseless waste can be traced to one and only one source, namely, lack of knowledge. Men and women who would not attempt to treat the slightest ailment, or even adjust so common a thing as a kitchen faucet, but would hand each difficulty over to its respective specialist, the doctor or the plumber, will on the spur of the moment and without the slightest preparation, undertake the investment of thousands of dollars in enterprises about which they understand absolutely nothing. Is it any wonder then that they lose?

I offer you suggestions and advice in the science of speculation and investment in the same spirit as the physician. He would not think of guaranteeing you perpetual life or insuring you against the common ills to which the flesh is heir. But in your difficulties he brings to your aid the accumulated experience of his profession, and a skill and knowledge which required years to accumulate and is ready for your instant use. I do not offer you a beautiful theory which will not work in practice, but give you invaluable advice, which if followed, will insure success in practical everyday Wall Street speculations and other fields of investment.

It has been well said that a writer who writes first for remuneration and secondly because he believes what he writes, will never achieve enduring fame, and that the salesman who does not believe in his goods will never make a success. I believe in the theory and rules that I have laid down in this book for you to follow, because I have tested and proved them.

It is my object in this work to facilitate and focalize the essential principles for practical use. My knowledge comes from over twenty years' experience, in which I have traversed the rough and rugged road that the inexperienced trader's foot must press before he reaches the goal. Hence my object in writing this book is to give to the public something new and practical, not theory alone which would fail in practice.

Read this book carefully several times; study each chart and subject thoroughly, and a new light and knowledge will come to you every time you read it.

If I succeed in teaching only a few to leave wild gambling alone and follow the path of conservative speculation and investment, my work will not have been in vain and I will have been amply repaid for my efforts.

W.D. GANN.

CONTENTS

BOOK I

PREPARATION FOR TRADING

BOOK II

HOW TO TRADE

BOOK III

HOW TO DETERMINE THE POSITION OF STOCKS

BOOK IV

COMMODITIES

CHARTS

Perhaps one of the wisest things Emerson ever said:

"Many times the reading of a book
has made the fortune of a man --
has decided his way in life.

"To use books rightly is to go to them for help;
to appeal to them when our knowledge and power fail;
to be led by them into wider sight and clear
conception of our own."

TRUTH OF THE STOCK TAPE

BOOK I

PREPARATION FOR TRADING

"No man can learn what he has not preparation for learning, however near to his eyes is the object. A chemist may tell his most precious secrets to a carpenter, and he shall be never the wiser -- the secrets he would not utter to a chemist for an estate." -- EMERSON.

In 1917 when the United States was forced to enter the war against Germany we heard on every hand "we are un-prepared for war." Wilson's period of "watchful waiting" instead of preparing for the inevitable had at last brought us face to face with war without being ready.

Lawyers, doctors, engineers and professional men who make a success spend anywhere from two to five years' time studying and preparing to practice their profession before they begin making any money.

Men enter into speculation in Wall Street without any preparation. They have made no study of it whatsoever. They try to deal in something they know nothing about. Is it any wonder then that they lose?

Speculators and investors who simply guess, follow tips, rumors, newspaper talk and so-called "inside information" have no chance of ever making a success. Unless they follow some well-defined plan based on Science and Supply and Demand, they are sure to lose.

Over twenty years of study and experience places me in a position to give you a definite, practical set of rules and instructions which will lead to success if you follow them.

No great success or gain can be expected unless a man is willing to study and learn by past experience. You cannot get something good for nothing and must pay with time, money, or knowledge for success.

CHAPTER I

WHAT IS TAPE READING?

Tape reading is a study of fluctuations of stocks as they appear on the stock tape and the ability to judge the ones that are in a strong or weak position and determine the psychological moment to buy or sell. We must also be able to determine the stocks that are inactive and show no definite trend.

Tape reading is psychological because the mind acts and is influenced by everything it sees, hears, smells, tastes or feels. In reading the tape, we are not influenced alone by what we see, but by what we feel or sense, which cannot always be explained or a satisfactory reason given because it is "intuition."

What is *intuition?* You often hear traders say "I am buying or selling this stock on my intuition. The best definition I can give of intuition is that it is *instantaneous reasoning.* It is that something which tells us when we are right or wrong before we have time to reason it out. The way to benefit through intuition is to act immediately, and not stop to reason or ask why. That is what a good tape reader does.

The tape registers the dominating force currents from business all over the country. It contains the condensed opinion of the majority and weighs the hopes and fears of manipulators, the public, and business men. That is why it is a reliable guide and business barometer, if you know how *to read it correctly.* And here is where the "rub" comes. *The tape tells the truth, if you can interpret it correctly.*

Tape reading requires a strong will power and a mind that, when it once sees the trend of the market, cannot be changed until the tape shows the change and is not influenced by news, false rumors, tips, or hearsay. Being able to read the tape correctly and act on your judgment is an entirely different proposition, which I will explain later on.

2

CHAPTER II

CAN MONEY BE MADE IN WALL STREET?

OR

CAN THE STOCK MARKET BE BEATEN?

You have often heard the expression "99 out of every 100 who go into Wall Street lose." Then one man out of every hundred must win. Therefore, my answer is that Wall Street can be beaten and that you can make money by speculating and investing along conservative lines and by trading in a few selected stocks.

But how are you going to do it? You must have knowledge and science. Know! Know !! Know!!! more than the other fellow or the common trader. Find out how successful men in Wall Street have made their fortunes; then go and do likewise. Remember that "Knowledge is Power."

Statistics show that 98 per cent of business men fail sooner or later. Then why do men go into business? Because 2 per cent of them make fortunes out of general business and keep them.

Just ask yourself the question, "Who gets all the money that is lost in Wall Street?" It does not evaporate; for every dollar lost some one makes a dollar. Then the way to make it is to trade the same way the fellow does who gets what you lose. Remember that every time you buy some one sells and every time you sell some one buys.

The majority of people who buy stocks lose money in the end. Why? Because they guess, follow newspaper dope, fake tips or inside information. They do not make safe investments; they gamble on 10 or 15 points' margin. They nearly always buy near the top, and, of course, nothing can keep them from losing.

The general public do not sell stocks short; therefore they are always wrong in a Bear market. When a man loses money buying stocks and refuses to sell short, he can always look back and say "if I had only sold when I bought, look how much profit I would have made." Then, why doesn't he learn to sell short? (In another chapter I will show you the proof that it is safe and practical to sell short.)

At the present time, there are over 700 stocks listed on the New York Stock Exchange, and if you group them under their proper headings, there will be over 20 different groups. If you study the action of all the stocks in one group and watch them on the tape, you will find it is too much for you, and that you cannot make money trading in all of the stocks in any one group, much less by trying to trade in several groups.

Tape reading requires *patience,* and the essence and value of it is *concentration.* There is no such thing as a man being born with a mind that can concentrate on 10 things at one time, much less 700. Then *success* depends upon *selecting* a *few stocks* and *concentrating* upon them.

CHAPTER III

HOW TO READ THE STOCK TAPE

The general opinion prevails with the public, especially among traders outside New York City, that the proper way to read the tape is to stand at the ticker and watch every quotation as it comes out. Nothing is more erroneous.

Expert tape readers are very few and far between. It is a study of a lifetime. While the tape shows the trend of the market, there are so many minor changes and quick reversals that the average man can not tell whether the big trend has turned or whether it is only a minor change that will last a few hours, a few days, or a few weeks before the main trend is resumed again.

If a trader goes into a broker's office to watch the tape, he will find anywhere from two or three to a dozen traders standing around the ticker, all talking from time to time and expressing their opinions or what they hear on different stocks. He must also listen to the gossip that comes over the news ticker, floating rumors from the street, and information about buyers and sellers that comes from the floor. With all of these disturbances, there is not one man in a million that can concentrate enough to tell anything about what stocks are going to do.

Besides, if he is able to pick a winner, and starts to buy or sell, he will be influenced by what someone says who is standing around the ticker and the result is that he will not act at the right time. Then it is impossible to beat the market by tape reading in a broker's office.

No matter how strong a man's will power may be, he is influenced, consciously or unconsciously, by what he hears or sees, and his actions or executions are interfered with accordingly. This is the reason why a few big traders, like Livermore, have a private office with a ticker, where they can be

5

away from all outside influences and watch the tape, form their impressions, and act on them without being influenced by things they do not want to hear. But only traders who have a very large amount of money and can devote all of their time to the market and tape reading can afford to have an office and a ticker where they can study the tape alone without interference. The average man cannot afford this.

Then it is *necessary* to *know how* to *read* the *tape without seeing it,* or without watching it all the time. Market movements of importance, i.e., the long swings, require weeks and sometimes months to get ready, or for accumulation and distribution to be completed. There is always plenty of time to buy or sell one or two days after a big move gets under way. Therefore it is not necessary to watch the tape every day, or every hour, in order to determine what stocks are going to do. It can be read just as easy and better after the market closes. The tape is simply a record of prices, and if you have this record of high and low prices made during the day, you can form your judgments from it.

Market movements depend upon Supply and Demand. It requires volume of trading in proportionate large or small amounts to move stocks up or down. The volume of sales to the stock market is the same as the steam is to the locomotive or the gasoline is to the automobile. The sales are the motive power which drives prices up or down.

For example: United States Steel has five million shares of common stock, and it requires a very large volume of sales to move this stock up or down very much. General Motors has fifty million shares of common stock and its fluctuations are confined to a very narrow range, because the buying or selling of 100,000 shares will not move it more than a point, if that much, while the buying of 100,000 shares of Baldwin will often move it up or down five or ten points, because there are only 200,000 shares of Baldwin outstanding and seldom ever over 100,000 shares of stock floating in the street.

Therefore, in order to understand the meaning of volume, you must know the total capital stock outstanding and the floating supply of the stock you are trading in. Mex Pete for several years has made moves of from 50 to 100 points while U. S. Steel has not moved 10. The reason was that the floating supply of Mex Pete was very small while the floating supply of U. S. Steel was very large.

Another thing the tape reader must know is the financial position of the stock, whether it is weak or strong. It is not easy to frighten investors and traders and start a selling move in a stock which is generally known to be in a very strong financial position. Neither is it easy to force a stock by manipulation to very high levels that is generally known to have very little intrinsic value. Many stocks, known as *"Mystery Stocks,"* which are supposed to have large concealed assets, often have big moves up or down because the public buy or sell on the hope that something favorable is going to happen or on the fear that something unfavorable is going to happen.

As a rule, a stock that pays extra dividends or cuts a melon, is talked about and rumors circulated months and even years before the actual event takes place. Then, of course, when the good news comes out, it has been anticipated and discounted and the stock declines instead of advancing, as the public expect.

The tape is the great scale in which the weight of all buying and selling is weighed and the balance of Supply and Demand shown by the loss or gain in prices. When *Supply exceeds Demand, prices decline* to a level where Supply and Demand are about equal. At this stage fluctuations become narrow and it may require weeks or months to determine which way the next move will be. When *Demand exceeds Supply, prices advance.*

Then how can the man who stands over the ticker day by day determine a big move before it starts? He can not. The ticker will fool him once or twice each day while it is getting ready. It requires time to buy a large amount of stock when accumulation is taking place, and it requires time to distribute a large amount of stock at the top. One day, one week, or one month is not enough for a big move. Sometimes it requires several months, or even a year, to complete accumulation or distribution. While this process is going on, you can keep up a chart of the stock you are interested in and judge much better when the big move starts, than you can by *watching* the *ticker every day.*

CHAPTER IV

HOW THE TAPE FOOLS YOU

The tape is used to fool traders, for often when stocks look the weakest on the tape, they are the strongest as accumulation is taking place. At other times when they are booming and very active and appear the strongest, they are really the weakest, because the insiders are selling while everybody is enthusiastic and buying.

The man who watches the tape daily is influenced by his hopes and fears. He can not help it. Suppose that the market has been strong all day, and the very stocks that he is interested in are gradually moving up, when suddenly, around 2:30 P.M. the market starts to break. It goes down for fifteen minutes and active stocks are off a point from the highs all around. It does not rally and by five minutes to 3, or closing time, they are off another point. The volume is heavy and he decides that something is wrong and he sells out at the close. The next morning stocks open up from 1/2 to 1 point. Why? Because the selling in the last half hour the day before was simply the result of profit taking and all of the traders who were scared sold out at the close rather than carry them over night, the result being that the supply of stocks to be offered next morning was limited, and the reaction had in no way interfered with or changed the main trend.

One great mistake the man makes who watches the ticker all the time, is that *he trades too often.* He gets in and out sometimes several times during the day, and each time he pays commission. If he buys or sells higher or lower each time, even though he has made profits on his trades, he is increasing the percentage against him. A man who makes 300 trades in the year, or, say, one for each market day, must pay an average of 1/2 point getting in and out. It cannot be done for less. Then 1/2 point on 100 shares 300 times, is 150 points for expenses during the year. Where is the man who can make money with such a handicap? Suppose a man makes one trade each month, or twelve trades during the year. His expenses are only six points against the scalper's expense of 150.

Another important fact traders overlook is that the more times a man gets in or out of a market, the more times he changes his judgment. Therefore, the percentage of his being wrong increases. In a bull or bear market, there are often big reverse moves opposite to the main trend, from which big profits can be made, but a man can not catch them by jumping in and out every day. He must wait until he has a real cause and sufficient reasons, based on facts, before he makes a trade. If he jumps in or out on hope or fear, he will not only *make losses,* but he *will miss* the *real oppor-tunity when it comes.* The daily moves generally mean very little to the main trend of the market.

OVERNIGHT BUYING OR SELLING ORDERS

As a rule, out-of-town buying orders accumulate over night. If the buying orders are in excess of the selling, stocks will advance for the first thirty minutes, while the public's buying orders are being filled. Then a reaction will take place. Prices may go lower than they were at the opening; drift along in an uncertain way until about 2 :30 P.M. when the professional crowd on the floor decide to even up; then either advance or decline for thirty minutes, according to whether the floor traders are long or short.

Remember that the professional floor traders have no commission to pay. You can buy a stock that goes up 1/2 point; then sell out and you are just about even, after paying taxes and commission, while the scalper on the floor makes 1/2 point, because he saves the commission.

The newspapers on Sundays usually carry a review of the market for the past week and the public, after reading all of the news, send in their buying and selling orders for Monday morning. If the orders are very heavy, they will influence the market for thirty minutes and sometimes one hour. After this, the trend of the market will be the opposite.

A market that has been strong during the week or especially during the latter part of the week and closes strong on Saturday, is likely to open strong Monday and finish the advance in the first hour on Monday. Therefore, be very careful about buying stocks on Monday morning's strong opening. Public buying orders which accumulate over Sunday are all executed Monday morning and as soon as this demand is supplied professionals start selling and the market has a reaction in proportion to its condition and position at the time.

Even if it is a bull market and going higher you will be able to buy cheaper on Monday afternoon or Tuesday when the professionals are hammering prices down after the public buying wave has been satisfied.

The above rule is reversed in a declining market. If stocks have been weak all the week or during the last two or three days of the week, and close at the low on Saturday, forced selling by the public will come in Monday morning and cause lower prices during the first 30 minutes to one hour. After this pressure is off, the market will rally. Therefore, it pays to sell on a strong rally Monday or to buy on a weak market on Monday morning. This rule of course applies to normal markets.

FALSE HOPES

Another point, when a man is long or short of the market, and has a loss, it is but human nature to hope that the trade will go his way. Suppose he is called for margin early in the day. He tells his broker that he will either put up the margin before the close or sell out his stocks. The result is he waits all day, and the market fails to rally. The last hour comes, and hope gives away to despair and he sells out at the close, which causes the market to close weak and near the bottom, because hundreds of people are doing the same thing at the same time.

The same rule applies to people who are short of the market. Stocks start advancing early in the day, and they wait for a reaction on which to cover. They look for a reaction around the noon hour, but it fails to come. Again around 2 :oo P.M. the market is stronger, and they hope for a reaction, but the advance continues, with the result that near the close all of the shorts get frightened and buy in their stocks. Of course, the market closes on top and is left in a weak technical position, and the next day the reaction comes.

For a trader to succeed, he must study human nature and do the opposite of what he finds the general public does. The first day of a decline no one worries much, because they consider it a natural reaction. A market will often start declining on Wednesday. On Thursday the decline continues, and the traders begin to sit up and take notice and think they had better get out on the next rally. But Friday comes, and no rally; instead stocks get weaker. Why? Because people who would not sell on the first or second day of the decline begin to sell on the third day, and by Saturday the whole crowd gets scared and decides to get out and not go over Sunday. The result is that prices will break badly in the last hour and close near the bottom, while the wise trader or tape reader who knew his business sold on the first indication of weakness the first day and did not wait until everybody was selling.

This same rule applies to declines and advances lasting weeks or months. The longer the market goes one way or the other the greater the buying or selling in the last stage, because *hope* or *fear increases* as the market *advances* or *declines,* and it is *hope* and *fear, not sound judgment,* that most people trade on.

STOCKS DISCOUNT FUTURE EVENTS

The stock market is an accurate barometer of business conditions. Stock prices are nearly always six to twelve months ahead of business conditions. First bond prices rise; second stocks advance; third comes business boom. The same happens in a decline. Stocks will be down six to eight months while business is booming, because they are discounting the future business depression.

Market movements, that is, the main swings, are the

result or effect of causes which, as a rule, exist long before
the effect is known to the general public. In most cases, news
is discounted before it comes out and seldom has much effect
after it is generally known. Either good or bad news that
is expected usually falls flat as far as the effect on the market
is concerned.

For instance, an extremely good or bad quarterly or
annual report on a stock comes out and the market does not
go up or down on it for the reason that it is not news to
those on the inside. They knew it thirty to ninety days beforehand. Therefore, when the public gets the news and acts
on it, it is too late, for those on the inside who "know" have
already discounted it.

If bad news comes out suddenly and stocks start selling
off in large volume, then it is safe to assume that the market
is going lower, that the public is long of stocks and the
insiders are out. If good news appears and stocks start
down, it shows that it has been discounted. Your charts
will show whether the market is in a period of distribution
or accumulation.

SUDDEN UNEXPECTED NEWS

Sometimes sudden, unexpected events happen unforeseen.
For instance; the earthquake in San Francisco in 1906 was
wholly unexpected and unforeseen by either the public or the
insiders. It caused great loss and damage to property, and
the market started breaking immediately after it, and declined for several weeks until it discounted the damage done
to the various properties affected in that territory. When
news of this kind comes out, that the market has not had
time to prepare for, its full weight and effect must be felt
after it comes out.

On February 3, 1917 Germany suddenly and without
warning declared the U-Boat war against the United States.
The stock market had not fully discounted this event because
neither the general public nor the insiders knew it was coming.
Once the news was out, everyone knew that it meant that the
United States must enter the war against Germany. Therefore, it was bad news which had not been fully discounted

and the market had yet to measure its effect. The result was that stocks opened off anywhere from 5 to 20 points, but supporting orders had been placed and the buying by shorts afforded enough support to stop the decline in the first hour of trading.

When a move of this kind occurs and a market opens away up or down, making a wide range, it is always well to sell out long stocks or cover shorts and wait, because in doing this you are following what the big traders do. On February 3rd, after you saw the market open down on heavy selling and you watched it for thirty minutes and saw that prices did not get much lower than the opening, it would be an indication that prices had opened at a level where there was support and that a rally would come. If you were short, the proper thing to do would be to cover at the market, then wait and see how stocks acted on the rally that day and the following day. If the rally was small and stocks again declined easily and began to break the low levels made on the day the bad news came out, it would be an indication that prices were going lower.

ELECTIONS

You will find it of great value if you will go back over the years of Presidential elections and study the action of the market and the formation of it on the chart in the early part of the year and again just previous to the election and following it. In most cases you will find that the event, whether considered good or bad, was discounted beforehand.

There is seldom ever a presidential year but what at some time there is a scare and severe decline. Public senti-ment gets mixed. They decide the Democrats are going to win and the market starts in to discount it. However, it makes no difference whether there is a Democratic president or a Republican. If stocks have been distributed and are in the hands of the public, they will go down during a Repub-lican administration. We have had just as many panics when a Republican president occupied the White House, as have occurred when the Democrats were in power. It all depends upon at what level prices are, and the condition of affairs throughout the country. This will be plainly registered by the tape and your chart will show it. If not, wait until you get a clear indication.

An extreme decline occurred in July and August, 1896, which was known as the "Silver Panic." The whole country got scared and decided that Wm. J. Bryan was going to be elected and that his silver dream would become a reality. Investors and traders sold stocks regardless of value and on August 8th, the average prices of industrial and railroad stocks reached a level which was the lowest from that day until the date of this writing.

In 1912, when Wilson was elected for the first time, the stock market advanced in September and October previous to the election, because the Republicans were convinced that the Democrats would not win. Therefore, they did not create any scare to start the public selling stocks. Of course, after Wilson was elected, which really was an unexpected event to investors who believed and feared that the "d----- Democrats" would ruin the country, they then began to sell stocks and discount the Democratic administration. The war followed in 1914 and completed the liquidation and made it even worse than it would have been. But this decline in stocks would have taken place even though a Republican had been in power, for the good and sufficient reason that prices were high, and that stocks had passed from strong hands into weak, and the general condition of the country was not such as to warrant the existing level of values at the time of the election.

AFTER-ELECTION RALLIES

When any important election, either presidential or otherwise, takes place, and the market has pretty well discounted it, but the general public throughout the country figure that the event is favorable, they, of course, send in buying orders the next day after election and stocks are strong until this demand is satisfied. It will always pay you to wait two or three days after election and see whether the market continues to move in the same direction after election as it did before. Stocks were strong the first day after

Wilson was elected the first time, but the decline started promptly after public buying orders had been filled. Always be careful of buying on top of after-election rallies. In the same way, if stocks open off and decline the first two or three days after election, be careful about selling them, as it may be only the public selling because they are scared and the insiders may support the market and start an advance.

CHAPTER V

HOW STOCKS ARE SOLD

When new companies are formed and capital is needed, the stock has to be sold to the public, and there is no difference in the method of selling stock and the method used by business men in selling their goods. A good business man advertises his goods and that is what the manipulators do. When they wish to distribute stocks and get them into the hands of the public, they use the newspapers in every way possible to advertise the stock. Their fluctuations are given wide publicity and everything possible is done to attract the public.

It requires wide fluctuations and activity to entice the public to take a hand. They may pay very little attention to a stock selling around 40 when it is only fluctuating 5 or 6 points in three or four months, but when this same stock reaches 150 and begins to fluctuate 5 and 10 points each day, everybody talks about it. They see great opportunities for making big profits and begin to trade in it. The result is that the wide publicity and advertising induces the public to buy all the stock at a high price. Then the decline starts. They hold on and hope, and nothing much is said about it until the stock gets near the bottom, when all the bad news comes out and everybody talks about it.

THE WISH IS FATHER TO THE THOUGHT

When you read the opinion of any man, whether it be a newspaper writer, the president of some big bank or the head of some large corporation, consider and give due weight to the fact that when he talks optimistic, he has something to sell to the public and is not likely to talk in a way to hurt his own business.

Many years ago there was a Mr. B. in Wall Street who gathered a lot of information and sometimes wrote for the newspapers. He was well known and often visited different brokerage offices, and traders eagerly sought his opinion. They would say "Mr. B., what do you think of Union Pacific?" He would reply: "I think it is going up; anyway, I hope it does, for I am long of it." Now, that was his reason for thinking the stock would go up. He owned some of it, and his hope and wish was that it would advance. He certainly did not feel like telling the other fellow that he believed it was going down. If he did, he might start a selling wave that would hurt his own interest.

OVER-OPTIMISM

If you have read the newspapers carefully over a long period of years, or if you will go back and look up records, you will find that prominent business men who are heads of large corporations, are nearly always optimistic. Panics come, and depressions lasting from one to five years, with stocks declining anywhere from 25 to over 100 points, yet these men are always optimistic. Do you believe that they are so far wrong in their judgment that they can not see the trend at the time? Certainly not. They have goods to sell. They must conceal it from the public and talk for their own interests.

I can not recall the time when the officials of the U. S. Steel Corporation were ever pessimistic. Yet, the stock has passed its dividend several times and suffered severe depressions, which as far as the records are concerned, were all unforeseen by the directors.

It is a good thing to be an optimist, but whether it be in business or the stock market, it is the truth that helps and protects, and not false hopes and unwarranted optimism. Hopes will not keep the margin call away from you in a panic. The only way to avoid these uncomfortable conditions is to go with the trend of the market and not against it.

The newspapers, as a rule, are against printing anything of a pessimistic nature. In 1920 and 1921 when I issued my forecast on general business conditions, I had based it on the truth and scientific facts. It showed that very depressing conditions were coming in 1920 and 1921, but most of the newspapers refused to publish my predictions. Yet they were all fulfilled with remarkable accuracy.

Forewarned is forearmed! It is certainly better to tell the public before depressing conditions start that they are coming and let them prepare for them, than to wait until the crisis is on and then tell them -- as the newspapers do -- what caused all the trouble. Every effect is the result of a cause, and the cause must exist long before the effect can be seen by the general public. The proper thing to do is to determine the cause and act on it, for if you wait until you can see the effect, loss in the stock market is certain.

TRADERS APE

After a man has been around Wall Street for twenty years and watches the actions of traders and listens to what they talk about, he will be convinced that the origin of man was certainly from the monkey or the ape, because the average trader simply apes some leader, repeats what he heard some great man say, believes it and applies it to his own case to increase his hopes or assuage his fears.

The late Mr. Morgan once said, "A man who is a bear on this country will go broke." I have often heard traders in a brokerage office talking bullish and buying, say, when a conservative man would warn them that bulls sometimes make money and bears sometimes make money but that a hog never makes anything: "Don't sell stocks short. A man who is a bear on this country will go broke." When Mr. Morgan, whose opinion as a business man is worthy of respect, made this statement, he was not talking about the stock market at all. If he had been, he would have said that the man who is a bull at the top of markets, which occur every few years, is sure to go broke, and the man who is a bear at the bottom is sure to go broke.

If traders would only use a little "horse sense" and do their own thinking, stop aping and swallowing all the newspapers tell them and analyze the reason or the motive behind the men who talk optimistic at the top and pessimistic at the bottom, they would make a great deal more money. To make success in the stock market you must do your own studying and thinking. Be neither a bull nor a bear, and no matter whose opinion you follow, you will be much better off if you can verify it by your own study of charts, which show the conditions as revealed by the tape, and the thoughts and opinions registered by the majority, and not the opinion of one man or one group of men, no matter how strong they may be.

The Standard Oil interests might be very bullish, and talk bullish. They might be honest and conscientious about it, and might be backing up their opinions by buying Standard Oil stocks, but the tape will register the buying and selling of all the people in the United States, and if that force of supply and demand shows that the selling of the many is greater than the buying of the few, the stock will decline until it reaches a level where demand exceeds supply.

SIGNS OF THE TIMES

The Bible says "There is a time for everything." All the laws of Nature teach this. There is a time to sow and a time to reap. The four seasons of the year teach us that there is a reaping time and a sowing time, and that we can not reverse this order of Nature's laws. Man does not try to grow oranges on Greenland's icy mountains; neither does he expect to cut ice from the tropical rivers in Florida, because it is out of season, time, and place. It is the same with the stock market. There is a time to buy and a time to sell, and when this time comes, neither bunches of bears nor bevys of bulls with hot air, hope, optimism, extreme pessimism, depression or bad reports, can force prices above or below the zones of Supply and Demand, out of season. You must learn to go with the tide, and not against it. Discern the signs of the times, and do not get caught in the undertow when the tide is flowing out. Those who hesitate and are late in buying or selling in the last stage invariably have to take losses.

CHAPTER VI

YOUR WEAK POINTS

Man know thyself! It has been well said that the greatest study of mankind is man. Experience is the only school in which most of us learn. Therefore it is necessary to analyze the cause of our mistakes much more carefully than our successes. A great success, either in business or the stock market, is not attained over night.

> "The heights by great men reached and kept
> Were not attained by single flight,
> But they while their companions slept
> Were toiling upward in the night."

Mushroom growth is followed by mushroom decay. A man who suddenly becomes wealthy over night or by a master lucky stroke in the stock market, seldom keeps it. It is the old story: "Easy come, easy go." The man who makes a success and keeps his money is the man who, after years of experience, has profited by his mistakes and schooled himself against his weak points.

To make a success in speculation, you must master yourself. You will find that you are either a natural born Bull or a natural born Bear, i.e., you either always hope and believe that stocks will go higher than they do, or you hope and believe that they will decline lower than they do. Then, you must discount your weak points in trading, and know that a lot of your judgment is not judgment at all, but the result of your natural weakness or inclination for one side or the other. Learn to see things in a normal state and do not exaggerate either on the bull or bear side.

Some men will find that they have too much nerve; are too hopeful; therefore they overtrade. Others will find that they lack nerve or courage and are afraid to buy or sell

enough at the right time. These weak points must be overcome. You must learn to trade so that there will be no hope
and no fear when you enter the market. You enter it as the
result of deliberation and upon what you believe to be the
proper basis for buying or selling. But you must remember
that you can be wrong and that the way to *protect yourself
against wrong judgment* is to *place a stop loss order at the
time you make the trade.* Then you do not have to hope it
will go your way or fear that it will go against you, for you
know that your loss is limited, and if the loss comes, you will
be in a position to make another trade later which will probably prove profitable.

CHAPTER VII

ESSENTIAL QUALIFICATIONS

PATIENCE

Patience is a virtue, especially in the stock market. Acquire it if you can. You must have patience to wait for the right opportunity to come, and not be overanxious and get in too soon. Once you buy or sell a stock and it starts moving in your favor, you must have patience to hold it until there is a good reason or sufficient cause for closing the trade. Never close a trade just because you have a profit; do not become impatient and get out for no real reason. Every act, either in opening or closing a trade, must have a sound basic cause behind it. Hopes and fears must be eliminated. There is no use selling a stock because you fear it is going down, nor buying it because you hope it is going up. Look at your charts and see which way the trend points and follow it. If no definite trend is shown, use your patience and wait.

NERVE

Nerve is just as essential as patience; in fact, nerve is the equal of capital. In getting my experience, I have been broke over 40 times, i.e., I have lost all of my money, but there never has been a time yet when I lost my nerve. Years ago, when I was experimenting and working on methods for forecasting the market, I would get in the market wrong and lose all my working capital, but I never let it get my "goat." I studied very carefully how I made the mistake and what the cause of the loss was. In this way, I profited by every mistake and loss, and was enabled to perfect my method of forecasting and trading so that I could make a success.

Looking backward brings nothing but regrets. I always
believe in facing the future with nerve and hope. But let
the nerve and the hope be based on some sound principle
that will prevent costly mistakes of the past. During my
career I have seen many traders who had made one mistake
after another and suffered severe losses, and still had some
capital to work with but when an opportunity appeared, they
lacked the nerve to act. In cases of this kind, the nerve
would have been more valuable than capital.

KNOWLEDGE

In the early part of my career I made some great successes, and what might be called lucky strikes. I made a lot
of money easily and then I spent or lost it easily. But I did
not give up or lose my nerve. I always figured that I was
a better man after each reverse, because I had acquired
experience.

Experience is the only school to learn in and the burnt
child is the one who knows the pain from having put his
fingers in the fire. Mistakes are all right and hard to avoid.
They are good for us, because if we profit by them, they
prove valuable. But it is wrong to make the same mistake
the second time. Therefore, use every mistake as a stepping
stone to progress; analyze each mistake you make and the
cause of every loss, in order to avoid repeating the same
error in future.

With each experience I had, good or bad, I accumulated
knowledge, and after all, knowledge is the greatest power
of all, for capital will always come to knowledge. Several
years ago a brokerage failure occurred suddenly and unexpectedly, and I lost all of my money. To the ordinary man's
way of figuring I was broke, but as a friend of mine expressed
it at the time, "He may be without cash, but the knowledge
that he has of the stock market is worth hundreds of thousands of dollars and in a short time he will turn that knowledge into cash." I did come back quickly in a few months'
time on a small capital, because I had a greater knowledge
of the stock market than ever before, and knowing, by experience, that I had a method based upon mathematical

science which could be depended upon to forecast the stock market, I had the nerve to pyramid and press the market hard when my science showed that I was on the right side. What would have been the result had I been without knowledge and only filled with hope? I would have stayed broke, as other traders do who follow the fairy phantom of "hope" in Wall Street trading.

HEALTH AND REST

Good health is essential to success in any line. It is one of the great assets for success in the speculative market. At least twice a year a man should close up all of his trades, get entirely out of the market, and go away for a vacation or stay away from the market and rest up. Let your mind rest and your judgment get clear. The man who continually sticks to any business too long without a rest or change gets his judgment warped. He gets in a rut and sees things from a one-sided point of view.

When you are in the market on either side, it is but human nature for you to hope that it will go your way, and you, therefore, give greater weight to any event that seems to indicate a favorable move to your side. When you are out of the market, you are able to see things as they really are, and judge the market without a distorted view, with hope and fear eliminated. Traders who are continually in the market day in and day out and never allow any time to elapse between trades, sooner or later lose all their money.

I know one trader who follows scientific forecasting and makes a success. He never makes more than five or six trades in the year. If he buys stocks during the winter or early spring for a rise, and the advance materializes as he expected, he sells out and takes his profits. Then he leaves the market alone, sometimes for several months. In the summer, if he sees indications of a bull or a hear market starting, he gets in again, and if the market moves his way, he may follow it up and pyramid for several months. When he gets an indication that the end is near, he closes up his trades, takes his profits, and like the wild geese, wends his way to the sunny South. Sometimes he stays all winter in

Florida, hunting and fishing; then goes over to Hot Springs, Arkansas, takes a course of baths; returns to Wall Street in good health and fit for another tilt with the Bulls and Bears.

He makes a specialty of trading in certain favorite stocks. He studies them closely and watches for certain signs that he considers almost infallible. When these signs come, he acts. He does not hurry until the time comes, but when it does, then there is no hesitation -- he buys or sells. He keeps cool, calm and collected, and waits for the time to open or close a trade.

Another thing he never does is to expect any fixed amount of profits or set any specific time for getting out. I have often seen him make a trade and it would go against him. He would get out and say, "Well, I guess I'll go back to my office and watch them for awhile." Sometimes it would be days or weeks before he made another trade, but when he did, it was based on some good sound reason, and 90 per cent of the time the second trade proved a winner. But suppose he had held the first trade he made and hoped it would move his way. His judgment, being biased, would have become more unreliable all the time. There is nothing like being out of the market and looking them over from an impartial viewpoint. When there is no definite trend, stay out, watch and wait, and your patience will be rewarded.

BOOK II

HOW TO TRADE

"The greatest achievement was at first and for a time a dream. The oak sleeps in the acorn; the bird waits in the egg; and in the highest vision of the soul a waking angel stirs. Dreams are the seedlings of realities." -- ALLEN.

Have a well-defined plan before you start trading, then follow that plan, as the architect does in building a house, or the engineer in constructing a bridge or driving a tunnel.

The man who changes his ideas or his plans, which are based on something practical, for no other reason than that he hopes or fears the market will do something different, will never make a success.

Don't guess or follow tips. Very few people from the inside ever give out good information. Have a reason for every trade; don't trade on hope. If that is the only reason or excuse you have for holding a stock, get out quickly and you will save money. Conditions change and you must learn to change your mind.

First find out if a rule is practical; if it is based on sound reasoning. Go back over past records and convince yourself that it pays to use it. The valuable part of the rules that I have laid down and the theory that I am teaching is that it can all be proved. You do not have to accept my word for it. Look up the records; examine the facts and satisfy yourself.

CHAPTER VIII

RULES FOR SUCCESSFUL TRADING

If you can not follow a rule, do not begin speculating or investing, as you are sure to lose.

Learn to adhere strictly to a rule or do not follow it at all.

The following rules should be carefully studied and applied in your trading:

1ST: CAPITAL REQUIRED

You would not try to run an automobile and start out to travel several hundred miles unless you knew how much gasoline it required to run a given number of miles. Yet, you go into speculation without knowing one of the most important things, -- the amount of capital required to succeed and make speculation a business.

Do not try to get rich in a few months or a year. A man certainly should be satisfied if he can acquire a competent fortune over a period of ten to twenty years. Often we have one year when a man with nerve and knowledge and a small amount of capital can make a fortune. I have been able to pile up enormous profits in a short time by pyramiding, but this can not be done continuously and I do not claim to be able to do it. What I am trying to teach you is a safe, sure way, which will yield more profits than any other business on earth if you will only be conservative and not make speculation a wild gamble.

A man may go into business and lose all of his money and then years pass before he has another opportunity to make a large amount of money in that or any other business. Yet, in the speculative markets opportunities return every

year, provided a man has studied enough to see them when
they appear. The chances for gain are so unusual and so
many great opportunities do come in Wall Street that the
average man gets greedy, gambles and does not wait between
times for the real opportunity.

People expect more profits in speculation than in any
other business. A man who would be satisfied with a return
of 25 per cent per year in a business is not satisfied if he
doubles his capital every month in Wall Street. Many people
are satisfied with 4 per cent in a savings bank, but when they
come to Wall Street and put up $1,000.00 they expect to
make $1,000.00 in two or three weeks. They are the people
who buy on a 10-point margin and always lose.

Do not expect the impossible in speculative markets.
Great and unusual opportunities, when you can start at the
bottom or top of a move, pyramid and make a fortune, occur
every few years. Two or three times each year, when stocks
are at the extreme high or low, there are opportunities for
making 10 to 40 points' profit.

You may think an average of 1/2 point a day, or 3 points
a week, is too small a profit to bother with. Yet, in 52 weeks
it would amount to 156 points, or $1,560.00 a year, on a
10-share trade. Make speculation a business, not a gamble.
Go into it to stay, not to gamble all on a few trades, lose and
quit. Be patient. If you can double $1,000.00 the first year
and keep doubling it for ten years, you would have over a
million dollars.

Active leading stocks make major moves of 10 to 40
points three to four times a year. If you are able to catch
half of these major moves on conservative trades, your
profits will be enormous. Do not try to catch all the minor
fluctuations. The inside manipulators themselves do not get
one-tenth of the minor fluctuations. Why should you expect to?

In beginning to trade in stocks the most important thing
to know is the amount of capital required. Many traders
make the mistake of thinking that about 10 points margin
is enough. Nothing is more erroneous. The man who starts
trading on 10 points' margin is gambling, not even making
safe, speculative ventures. When you start to trade use your

capital as you would in a business, and in such a conservative way that you can continue.

For trading in stocks selling at $100.00 per share or over, you should have $5,000.00 for each 100 shares you trade in; $2,500.00 for trading in stocks selling over $50.00; $1,500.00 for stocks selling around $25.00; $1,000.00 for stocks selling at $10.00 to $15.00. This amount of capital is not to margin stocks and let them run against you 10 to 30 points. It is to be used to make a large number of trades and pay small losses when they occur. You should always limit your loss on each trade to about 3 points and never more than 5 points.

If you have only $300.00 to start trading with, when you buy or sell a stock, place a 3-point stop loss order on it. This will allow you to make ten trades on your capital. Suppose you make five consecutive trades and lose, your capital will be half gone, but if on the next trade you are right and make 15-points' profit, you will regain all of your losses; or, if you make three trades with 5 points' profit, they would wipe out the losses of five trades with 3 point losses on each.

2ND: LIMIT YOUR RISK

A strong will power is just as essential as plenty of capital. If you have not the firmness, will power, and determination to *protect every trade with a stop loss order,* do not start trading, for you will fail.

I have often heard traders say "If I place a stop loss order at a certain point the market is sure to catch it." Yet they realize afterward that the stop loss order being caught was the best thing that could happen to them. There is nothing better than getting out quickly when you are wrong. The man who refuses to get out when he is wrong usually stays until his money is gone and the margin clerk sells him out.

A lot of people do not know *how to place a stop loss order* on a trade when they make it. A stop loss order is an order given to the broker that becomes a market order when the stock reaches the price at which it is placed. For example:

We will assume that you buy 100 shares of U. S. Steel
at 106. You feel that 2 points is enough to risk on the trade
And that if it declines to 104 you would sell it out. It is not
necessary for you to sit in a broker's office and watch the
ticker until Steel declines to 104 and then get up and tell
the broker to sell 100 Steel at the market. When you buy
the stock simply give your broker an order reading as follows:

Sell 100 U. S. Steel at 104 Stop G. T. C.

which means "good till cancelled." Now, suppose that Steel
declines to 104. When it reaches this price, your broker
sells 100 at the market. He may get 104 for it or he may
get 103 7/8 or 103 3/4, but you know that when it reaches this
price your stock will be sold. A broker can not guarantee
to sell your stock at the limit of your stop loss order, but he
does sell it immediately at the next best price after your stop
loss order price is reached.

Suppose that you sell U. S. Steel short at 106 instead of
buying it, and that you want to protect yourself against loss.
You give your broker an order to buy 100 U. S. Steel at 108
stop G. T. C. If it reaches this price, he buys in the stock.

If your stop is not reached and the market goes in your
favor, you must then cancel your stop loss order when you
close out your trade with a profit. You can, of course, give
a stop loss order good for one day, one week, or any specified
length of time, but the best way to place the order is G. T. C.;
then you do not have to worry about it.

3RD: OVERTRADING -- THE GREATEST EVIL

Overtrading is the cause of more losses than anything
else in Wall Street. The average man does not know how
much capital is required to make a success and he buys or
sells more than he should. Therefore he is forced to get out
of the market when his capital is nearly exhausted and probably misses opportunities for making profits. Make up your
mind how much loss you can afford before you make a trade
and not afterward.

Stick to small quantities. Be conservative. Do not over-trade, especially at the bottom or top of long moves. Fortunes are lost trying to catch the last 3 to 5 points in extreme moves. Keep cool. Avoid getting overconfident at tops and bottoms. Study your charts carefully and do not allow your judgment to be influenced by hope or fear.

Many a trader has started out trading in 10 shares and made a success because he started near top or bottom; then when the market had reached extreme, he began trading in 100-share lots and lost all of his profits and capital too, because he violated the conservative principle which helped him to make a success.

If you make *one trade* and it *starts to go against you, you are wrong. Then why buy or sell more to average a loss?* When things are getting worse, day by day in every way, why do your best to make them get worse in every way? Stop the loss before it is *eternally too late. Every trader should remember that the weakest point of all is overtrading, and the next, failing to place a stop loss order, and the third fatal mistake of all, averaging a loss. Eliminate these three mistakes and you will make a success. Cut short your losses,* let *your profits run,* pyramid or increase your buying or selling when the market is moving in your favor, not when it is going against you.

Remember that wild, active markets are brought about by feverish manipulation, and that they increase the imagination, exaggerate your hopes, and take away all sense of reason and proportion. Therefore, in extreme markets try to keep a cool head. Remember that all things come to an end, and that a train going 60 miles an hour will cause a greater smash-up if it leaves the track than one traveling 5 miles an hour. Therefore, in a wild runaway market, jump before she bumps, for you will never be able to get out once the crash comes. When everybody wants to sell, and no one wants to buy, profits run into losses fast.

The great bull market of 1919 shows plainly what happens when everybody gets crazy bullish, and can see no top in sight. This bull market reached a point where everybody was bullish and buying, and no one on the outside dared to sell short. It was one of the fastest markets in history. And what happened? When the "bubble busted" in the early days of November and the decline started, some stocks were off 50 to 60 points in two weeks' time, and the profits made during the whole campaign that year were wiped out in ten days. The man who waited for a rally to get out on after the move started down never had a chance, because everybody was trying to get out, and the further prices declined, the more people there were forced to sell out, with the result that the market got weaker as it declined lower.

4ᵀᴴ : NEVER LET A PROFIT RUN INTO A LOSS

More traders are ruined by violating this rule than any other, except overtrading. When you buy or sell a stock and it shows you a profit of 3 to 4 points, what is the sense or reason for ever risking any more of your capital on it? Place a stop loss order where you will get out even or better; then you have all to win and nothing to lose. If the trade continues to move in your favor, you can follow it up with a stop loss order.

People often buy or sell a stock and it shows them a good profit, but they are "hoggish," expect more, hold on and hope and let it run into a loss, which is very poor business, and the man who follows it will not succeed in the end. Always protect your principal in every way possible.

5ᵀᴴ: DON'T BUCK THE TREND

The way to make money is to determine the trend and then follow it. When you are in a Bear market and the long trend is down, it is always much safer to wait for rallies and sell short than to buy. If you are in a big Bear market where stocks are going to break from 50 to 200 points, you can miss the bottom several times on the way down and lose all of your capital.

The same applies to a Bull market. You should never sell short on an advancing market. It is better to wait for reactions and buy than to try to pick tops for selling. Big profits are made by going with the trend and not against it.

One of the most vital and important things for either an

investor or a trader to learn is to take a loss and take it
quickly. When you see that you are wrong there is no use
putting up more margin and holding on and hoping. If you
take a small loss quickly and get out of the market, your
judgment will be much better and you can see an opportunity
to get in again and make profits.

6ᵀᴴ: WHEN IN DOUBT GET OUT

When you buy or sell a stock and it does not act right
immediately or start to move in your favor within a reasonable length of time, get out of it. Your judgment gets worse
the longer you hold on and hope for the market to go your
way, and at extremes you always do the wrong thing. It is
much better to take a quick loss of 2, 3, or 5 points than to
hold on and hope and eventually take anywhere from a 10
to a 50-point loss.

Stocks are not going to stop going up or down once they
start just for your benefit. Always remember what Jim
Keene said: "If stocks won't go your way, you must go their
way." Always go with the tide; never buck it. If you were
on a railroad track and saw a train coming at 60 miles an
hour, would you stand there and hope that the train would
stop before it hit you, or would you hope that maybe you
could knock it off the track? Of course you wouldn't. You
would get out of the way and do it quick. You should do
the same thing in the stock market -- Get out; let them go
by, or get aboard and ride with them.

7ᵀᴴ: TRADE IN ACTIVE STOCKS

Always confine your trading to standard, active stocks
listed on the New York Stock Exchange. Outside stocks
have spurts, but the active leaders yield more profits in the
long run. Stocks traded in on the New York Stock Exchange
always have a good market and you can get in and out when
you want to. Ninety per cent of the unlisted and curb stocks
disappear sooner or later. Leave the pups, cats and dogs,
and mining stocks alone.

The same group of stocks over a long period of time do

not remain leaders. Changing conditions in the country cause certain groups to lead for a time, then become laggards, while new groups become public favorites and leaders.

It is the same thing with individual stocks of the different groups. As a rule, a stock that becomes a favorite and a leader will continue active anywhere from five to ten years. After this period of time, it will pass into the hands of investors and its activity will cease. Fluctuations will become narrow because investors do not jump in and out every day. They hold for a long time, and finally when they do start to sell out for some good reason, or get scared, then the old time leaders become active on the down side until liquidation has been completed.

Of course, the big money is always made in trading in stocks that fluctuate over a wide range. For this reason, you must always be on the lookout for a new leader that will give opportunities for making big profits. Be up-to-date, keep up with the new stocks as they are listed, watch their development, and you will be able to pick the new live leaders and discard the old, inactive stocks. Big money is made, not from dividends but from fluctuations, if you know how to trade quickly. That is why it pays to trade in active stocks that make a wide range. If you have to take a loss in stocks of this kind, you can make it back very quickly, because opportunities occur often.

8TH: EQUAL DISTRIBUTION OF RISK

There is an old saying, "Never put all of your eggs in one basket." And in the stock market it is a very good rule to follow. If you are in position to do so, select as many as four or five stocks, one from each of the different groups. Buy or sell in equal amounts.

Divide your capital up so that you can make seven to ten trades with it. Suppose you have $5,000.00. Trade in 100-share lots and limit risks to 3 to 5 points. You would be able to stand five or six consecutive losses and still have capital to work with. By letting your profits run one big profit will often wipe out four or five small losses. But, if you take big losses and small profits, you have no chance of gaining in the end.

   If you can only trade in 50 shares, take 10 shares each of five different stocks. Place stop loss orders on these trades from 3 to 5 points away, according to the indications on the stocks you are trading in. Two of these stocks may go against you and catch your stop while the other three may not. This will leave you part of your holdings and if they move in your favor, will make back your losses on the others and show profits.

   If you get into the market right and with a reason, records show that it very seldom occurs that you would get the stops caught on all of your stocks. You may not always make as much profit as you would to trade in one or two of the active, fast moving stocks, but you will be safer. That is my aim: To teach you safety; help you protect yourself and cut short your losses in every possible way and let your profits run.

9TH: FIXING A PRICE OR POINT TO BUY OR SELL

   The majority of people have a habit when they buy or sell a stock, of fixing in their minds a certain figure at which they expect to take profits. There is no reason or cause for this. It is simply a bad habit based on hope. When you make a trade, your object should be to make profits and there is no way that you can determine in advance how much profits you can expect on any one particular trade. The market itself determines the amount of your profit, and the thing that you must do is to be ready to get out and accept a profit whenever the trend changes and not before. Remember the market is not going to act to please you or go to certain figures just because you want to buy or sell at those figures.

   Many traders lose big profits by fixing the price at which they intend to sell. Stocks sometimes go within 2, 3 or 4 points of their selling price and start to decline. They hold on and hope. Just because it does not reach the point that they have fixed in their minds, they often hold on and hope until they lose all the profits and take a loss, refusing to see that the trend has changed. *Hope will ruin any man who follows it in the stock market.* To succeed you must *face facts,* and *facts* are often *cold* and *stubborn* and *do not agree* with your *hope,* but you must accept them for your own good.

In nearly every bull or bear campaign in the market the general public gets certain fixed points in their heads where stocks are going to make tops or bottoms. The newspapers talk about certain favorite stocks going to 100, 125, 150 or 175. Everybody gets the idea that these prices are going to be made and they become "hope" prices, but are never realized.

To illustrate this: During the fall of 1909, when the bull campaign in stocks was at its height and Steel common had advanced to around 90, the newspapers began to talk of 100 for "little Steel." The public all got the idea in their heads that Steel was sure to make 100 and that was the place they were going to sell and take profits. The writer predicted that Steel would advance to 94 7/8 and no higher, which it did, and he sold out, while the "hope" crowd held on and eventually took losses, for U. S. Steel declined eventually to 38. Several years later when it did reach 100, it was the place to buy and not to sell, for it immediately advanced to 129 3/4.

The man who tries to get the last point or the top or bottom eighth generally loses all his profits. You do not have to get in at the bottom and out at the top to make big money. All you have to do is to look over the list of the active leading stocks and you will find that they make moves of from 50 to 150 points between bottom and top every few years. Then, if you can get in after the stock has advanced 10 points from the bottom, and sell out within 10 points of the top, you certainly will be able to accumulate plenty of profits.

Never get the *idea* in your *head that you can or will hold* a *stock until it goes your way.* This is nothing but pure *stubbornness* and is *not based on any sound logic or reasoning.* In case of doubt, get out. Do not hesitate. Delays are always dangerous. Do as the insiders do: If they can not get what they want, they take what they can get; if the market will not take what they have to offer, they offer what it will take; if the market will not go their way, they go its way. A wise man changes his mind, a fool never.

10ᵀᴴ: WHEN TO TAKE PROFITS

Never close a trade just because you have a profit. The time to hold on is when the tide is running in your favor. When tempted to close a trade just because you have a profit ask yourself the questions: "Do I need the money?" "Is the move over?" "Do I have to sell?" "Why should I take profits?"

Look at your charts; do what they tell you. If they do not show a change in trend, wait. Protect profits with stop loss order, but do not take a profit too soon. This is just as bad as taking a loss too late. Patience to hold on when you are right and nerve to get out quickly when you are wrong will make a success.

11ᵀᴴ: ACCUMULATE A SURPLUS

A surplus must be accumulated before you increase your trading quantities. Margins are not to hold on with, only "lambs" do that. If big risks are required, do not make the trade. Wait for an opportunity when you can buy or sell and place a stop loss order 3 to 5 points away. It is financial suicide to take big losses when they can be prevented.

You must not expand until after you have made profits. Every important business concern carefully creates a surplus and is proud to publish it. No business is run without a loss at some time and a speculator or investor must expect losses. Therefore, he must create a surplus out of which he can pay losses and still continue to trade.

In very active markets, when trading in high priced stocks, as a rule it does not pay to take a loss amounting to more than two consecutive days' fluctuations. If stocks go against you two days, they are likely to go more. Take your loss out of your surplus and leave your capital unimpaired and wait for another opportunity.

12ᵀᴴ: BUYING FOR DIVIDENDS

A great many people make the mistake of always wanting to buy stocks that will pay dividends. Do not buy stocks just because they pay dividends, nor sell them because they do not. Often people hold stocks because they continue to pay big dividends, only to see their capital half or more wiped out; then the dividend is cut or passed altogether. Look to the protection of your capital, not for dividend returns. Trade for points of profit, not dividends. Fluctuations yield more money than dividends and you will be able to tell when stocks are being accumulated or distributed for an advance or a decline.

If a stock is selling very low or out of line according to the dividend it pays, there is probably something wrong and it is a better short sale than a purchase. If a stock is selling very high and pays no dividend, there is a reason for it and you should not sell it short. Probably it is going to pay a dividend or it is in a very strong position. Otherwise it would not be selling at a high price.

Manipulation for a time will force stocks above or below their intrinsic value, but in the end Supply and Demand govern the course of prices, and values are based on these factors. I intend to teach you how to tell when Supply and Demand show the place where you should buy or sell.

The word "dividend" means a division of profits or earnings, but often when you buy Curb or mining stocks the word means "divy," or that you divide up your capital with the other fellow and later lose all.

CHAPTER IX

METHODS OF OPERATING

After you have learned the rules for successful trading, it is then necessary to determine the best methods for operating either on the buying or selling side. All of these factors help you to overcome the weak points and enable you to make a better success.

BUYING OUTRIGHT

Many people think that the only safe and sure way to make money on stocks is by buying outright. This is a sad mistake and has caused many a trader to come to grief. Study the records of past movements and you will find ample proof of my statement. You need only to refer to the great depressions that have occurred during the past forty or fifty years to prove that it can cost the entire amount of the price you pay when buying outright, i.e., stocks will not only go down to nothing, but they can be assessed.

How many people have you heard say "I own my stocks outright; I have nothing to worry about." They are just the people who should worry. Every year many stocks go out of existence or are assessed. How do people know that they have the one safe, good stock on the list?

At present there are about 700 stocks listed on the New York Stock Exchange. In five or ten years from this time conditions may so change that over 25 per cent of these stocks will be worthless or have declined enough to ruin any man who buys them outright and holds them.

You must have something better than buying outright to protect you in order to make money. It is just as safe to trade on conservative margin, and you will make much greater profits when you know the right stock to buy or sell and the right time.

In the boom which culminated in the Fall of 1919, many stocks had advanced in nine months from 25 to over 100 points. Suppose people bought any of these stocks outright within 20 to 50 points of the top and held them through the decline of 1920 and 1921. Some stocks declined 100 to 180 points. There were no exceptions. All stocks suffered tremendous losses, and many of them will never sell again at the prices they reached in 1919.

The man who sold stocks short in 1919 and played the short side in 1920 and 1921 until the summer of 1921 was the man who made the money. Below I give you the high prices of some stocks in 1919 and the low prices in 1921, which will prove to you what can happen to a man who buys stocks outright and feels safe:

	High 1919	Low 1920 & 1921	Points decline
American Woolen	169 1/2	55 1/2	114
Am. Intern'l	132 1/4	21 1/4	111
Atlantic Gulf W. I	192 1/4	18	174 1/2
Crucible Steel	278 1/2	49	229 1/2
General Asphalt	160	32 1/2	127 1/2
Kelly Springfield	164	25 1/2	138 1/2
Mexican Pete	264	84 1/2	179 1/2
Republic Steel	145	41 1/8	103 7/8
Studebaker	151	37 3/4	113 1/4
Transcontinental Oil	62 5/8	5 5/8	57
U. S. Food	91 3/8	2 3/8	88 5/8
U. S. Rubber	143 3/4	40 1/2	103 1/4

Most all of the above stocks were still paying dividends when they had declined 25 to 50 points from the top and they no doubt looked attractive to a lot of people who bought them either on margin or outright. How many men will have the nerve to hold on when they see their capital shrink from 50 to 75 per cent? Very few of them, and a man would be a fool if he did.

This is another proof that you must place a stop loss order for your protection, because when a stock starts to go against you, it certainly can go enough to cost you all of your margin and exhaust your patience, causing you to sell out, probably just at a time when you should buy.

I have not picked 1919 as an exception of a Bull market
or 1920 and 1921 as exceptional Bear years, because they
are not. These same kind of declines have occurred in
1857, 1873, 1893, 1896, 1903, 1904, 1907, 1910, 1914,
and 1917, and they certainly will occur again. Therefore,
be a Bear in a Bear market and a Bull in a Bull market.

Don't forget the fact that when stocks start to go against
you, they can go a long way in either direction, and that the
man who buys outright near the top and thinks he is safe,
or the man who sells short near the bottom and puts up 50
points margin and thinks it is enough, can both be wiped out.

You might argue that a man who buys outright in panic
years near the bottom is perfectly safe and doing the right
thing. My answer is that the man who buys on margin at
the bottom of a panic is just as safe and can make more
money because he can carry more stock and I intend to teach
you how to tell when stocks reach top or bottom.

SELLING SHORT

I am not going to tell you that it pays to sell short; I
am going to prove it to you by indisputable records covering
over thirty years of market movements.

A lot of people trade in the market for years and never
seem to realize that there are two sides to it. I have often
heard people remark when stocks were declining fast, "I
can not sell short." The man who is a born Bull, chronic
to the core, will never succeed; neither will a chronic Bear
succeed any better. You must have no sentiment in the way
you make money in the market. Your aim and object should
be to make profits and you should have no choice of how you
make them, whether it be on the buying or selling side. The
Royal Road to Success is to be a Bear in a Bear market and
a Bull in a Bull market.

If you only trade on the Bull side of the market, you
have 50 per cent more against you than if you trade on both
sides. What chance has a Bull in Bear years or years of
panic and depression? He may buy near the bottom of a
break, but unless he grabs profits quick, he will soon have
losses; while the Bear who sell stocks short on every rally,

covers them on the breaks and waits for rallies to sell again, is sure to pile up big profits because he is going with the trend, which you must always do.

Study the charts and convince yourself that at the right time there is just as much money on the short side as there is on the long side. Then make up your mind, if you expect to succeed, that you will sell short when conditions warrant.

Your friends, brokers, and the newspapers tell you that it is dangerous to sell short; that there might be a "corner." The chances for a corner in a stock are about one in a thousand. There have been only two important corners in the last 30 years, -- Northern Pacific was cornered in 1901, when it went from 150 to 1000 per share; Stutz Motors was cornered in 1920 and advanced from around 200 to around 700.

Stocks are made to sell and the insiders sell them near the tops just as fast as they can. You are always safe in doing what the insiders do. Stocks with large capitalization are perfectly safe to sell short, because there is a large floating supply of stock and it is impossible to corner them.

The newspapers tell you what the insiders want you to know, not what you need to know. Watch the newspapers. When things are the worst and it is time to buy stocks, they never tell you anything about the good times that are coming, but when stocks are top and the insiders want to unload all they bought at the bottom, the newspapers tell you about dividends, extra dividends, melons, rights, and large earnings, when they should tell you that you are picking "lemons" and are getting "wrongs" not rights on your stock.

A wise man does not expect something good for nothing, and only fools expect the fellow who is on the inside of the game, playing against them, to tell them what he is doing.

The sentiment among brokers is always bullish near the top and bearish near the bottom. The average broker knows no more about the market than you do, and there is no reason why he should. His business is to buy and sell stocks for commissions. That is the way he makes his money, and a broker who does this well earns all you pay him. His business is too confusing. He hears too much on both sides of the market to make his judgment any good.

In December, 1920, when stocks were declining rapidly on two-million share days, the newspapers told you about high money, frozen credits, depression in business, unemployment, buying power reduced, people unable to buy luxuries, automobiles, etc. At this time Studebaker sold at 37 3/4, which was the bottom. It steadily advanced, and not much was said about it until it got above 100.

Now, for several months past, every few days the newspapers tell you about the wonderful earnings of Studebaker. Tips are all around Wall Street that Studebaker is going to 175 or 200 a share. Why tell the outsider all this good news now after Studebaker is up nearly 100 points, and what will be the story told to the suckers who buy the stock at present levels, when it again sells down around 50 or 60, which it will in the latter part of 1923 or 1924? It is the writer's opinion that the man who sells Studebaker and pays the dividend for the next year will make more money than the people who buy it and get the dividends. This applies to other stocks as well as Studebaker.

PYRAMIDING PROFITS

Many a trader has begun at the bottom of a Bull market to trade conservatively and accumulated a large amount of profits. Finally he begins to pyramid too heavily and too fast near the top, with the result that when the trend turns he gets caught overloaded and loses all the profits he has made and probably a lot of his capital. Sad experience has taught me that it is better to be safe than sorry. In speculation let "safety first" be your motto.

In trading, your first risk should be your greatest. Suppose on your first trade you risk 5 points, which, if lost, comes out of your capital. We will assume that the stock moves 5 points in your favor. You can then buy a second lot and place a stop loss order 5 points away, and if it is caught, you will still be only loser 5 points, because you will be even on your first trade.

Pyramiding all depends on where you get in on a stock, -- whether near the bottom when a move starts upward or near the top when it starts downward. On active stocks, as a rule, it is safe to pyramid every 10 points up or down, but you should decrease your trades and never increase them.

Suppose your first trade is 100 shares and the market advances 10 points; then you buy 50 shares and it advances 10 points more; you buy 30 shares and it advances 10 points more; you buy 20 shares and it advances 10 points more, and you buy 10 shares. After that every 10 points up you buy 10 shares more. In this way, if you follow up with a stop loss order, your profits will always increase while your risk will decrease. Your last trade may show a loss of 3 to 5 points according to how you get out on stop loss orders, but all of your other trades will show big profits. It is always safer to pyramid after a stock moves out of accumulation or distribution zones.

Learn to adhere strictly to a rule or do not follow it at all. One thing you must not overlook, that every time a stock moves in your favor 5 or 10 points, the chances against it moving further in your favor have decreased. This does not mean that the stock will not go a long way in your favor, but it is the percentage against you that must not be overlooked.

BUYING AND SELLING ON A SCALE

Many investors and traders have the idea that the only successful way to trade is to buy or sell on a scale up or down. I have never yet seen a scale method that would beat the market. Some one asked Russell Sage if he believed in buying on a scale. He said that there were only three men who had money enough to buy on a scale, -- Carnegie, Morgan and Rockefeller, and they had more sense than to do it.

A scale method will not work for the reason that you add to your holdings when the market is going against you, thus increasing your risk. If the market is going against you on the first trade and it looks like you are in wrong, the thing to do is to get out quickly and not buy or sell more. The time to take additional risk is when the market is moving in your favor, as shown in my pyramiding plan. It is all right to buy or sell more if you are doing it when you are making profits, but when you are trying to average, with losses piling up against you, you are sure to make a serious mistake, which will sooner or later cost all of your capital.

HEDGING IN STOCKS

Traders who buy a stock of one group and it starts to move against them, figure that they can even up by hedging or selling something short in another group. This very seldom pays. It is much better to take a loss and take it quickly on the trade that is going against you, and start a new deal.

There are some instances, or have been in the past, where rails and industrials spread apart and then come together again, but to make a play of this kind requires a long period of time. For example:

In November, 1919, when 20 industrial stocks were selling on an average of 119, the Dow-Jones 20 rails were selling at 82, the industrials being 37 points higher than the rails. The writer figured that the industrials would sell lower than the rails within two years, which they did. In August, 1921, the rails were selling at 70 and the industrials at 66, the rails being 4 points higher than the industrials, or a difference of 41 points in favor of the rails in 21 months.

Of course, a trader who sold the high-priced industrial stocks short and bought rails, even at the top in 1919, would have made money, but this is not the way to trade, for the rails declined about 18 points while industrials were declining 55 points.

Therefore, the proper way to trade would have been to keep short of industrials as long as the trend was down, and not do any hedging. The great fundamental rule that you must learn in order to be a success is to follow the trend of the market. If you can not determine a definite trend, get out and wait until you can. You can always make plenty of money after the trend is well defined.

FAILURE TO FOLLOW RULES

The long swings in the stock market last on an average of two years, or approximately 600 market days. If you stand at the ticker and watch the fluctuations, it will make you change your mind 1200 times in two years. Ninety per cent of the time you will be wrong, because you are not changing your mind for any good sound reason, but simply because a minor move, which may last but a few hours or a few days, has changed the appearance of the position of the stock to the man who views it from short range, standing over the ticker.

Every time you change your mind and change your position, you increase the percentage against you, because you are paying taxes, interest and commission. If you get in wrong, the ticker will keep you wrong because it will make some minor moves every few hours or every few days that will renew your hope and keep you in. On the other hand, if you are in right, and are watching the ticker daily, some of these minor moves that mean nothing will get you out and you will lose a good position. Then, you must realize that you have very little chance to make any money watching a ticker, changing your mind and being wrong 90 per cent of the time.

The *stock tape moves in mysterious ways* the *multitude to deceive,* because the public are *influenced* by their *hopes and fears*. They sell on fear and buy on hope, thus getting in or out near the top or bottom, while the man who trades on some well-defined plan buys when the public sells and sells when the public buys. The *stock market does not beat you. You beat yourself* by following your own weaknesses, by listening to the man who knows less than you know, by reading the newspapers, following the gossip of the Street, all of which is put out to influence you in the wrong direction.

When the average trader comes to Wall Street he is looking for information. He asks the bootblack "What do you think of the market?" He also inquires of the waiter in the hotels, the office boy, his broker, friends and strangers around the broker's office. I am conservative when I say that the average floating trader asks the opinion of 10 to 12 people every day, most of whom are all guessers and know no more about the market than he does. If their opinions agree with his, he considers it good information and follows it, and of course, loses money. If half of the people he talks to disagree with him, he probably does not act on his own judgment, and later finds that it was right. He says to himself "If I had only bought when I intended to, I would have made money, but I talked it over with the broker and the boys, and they convinced me that I was wrong."

"A wise man changes his mind, and a fool never." A wise man also investigates and then decides; a fool just decides. The man who is fixed in his opinions on stocks, either a born Bull or Bear, will never make any money. A man must always be of open mind, ready to change his mind and act quickly when he finds that there is a good reason to do so. In *Wall Street* the *man who does not change his mind will very shortly have no "change" to mind.*

I know of a trader now in Wall Street who is an old man, probably eighty years of age. He has made several small fortunes in his day and some of his big profits were made when he got in stocks that moved quickly 50 to 100 points. After that, he would lose all of the money that he had made, trying to catch another move where he could make 50 to 100 points quickly.

This man had been broke for several years prior to 1915. When the great war boom started, he got hold of a few hundred dollars capital and started buying stocks and pyramiding. He got in at the right time, on the right stocks, i.e., he bought near the bottom; stocks began to advance and he began to pyramid. He bought Baldwin below 50, Crucible Steel below 40, Beth. Steel below 50, Studebaker below 60. He was fortunate enough to get into the real "war babies."

He was trading in odd lots in the beginning and when the market reached top in the fall of 1915, he was carrying thousands of shares. His equity with the broker was over $200,000. I said to him "Now is the time to turn your paper profits into cash." At that time Baldwin showed him over 100 points' profit, Crucible over 100 points and Beth. Steel several hundred points' profit on his original trades. But he had gotten so bullish and so full of hope that he thought everybody was crazy and that every stock on the list was going to be a Beth. Steel and go up to 700.

I remember one day in October, 1915, when Baldwin advanced to 154, which was the top, and the market was very wild and excited. I said to him "Now either sell out

all of your stocks or protect your profits with close stop loss
orders." He said "Stocks haven't started to go up good
yet" and he gave me an order to buy 500 more Baldwin.
He said "I am going to sell Baldwin around 250, not 150."
That afternoon Baldwin declined to 130, and all of his other
stocks in proportion, but he held on and hoped. Stocks continued to go down, and in a few months Baldwin was back
around 100 and he was forced to sell out his big line of
stocks, and his profits of $200,000 were reduced to where
his account showed less than $10,000.

Now, where is the mistake with this kind of trading?
This man saw the opportunity at the right time. He bought
small amounts of stocks at the right time and he pyramided
right. But he failed to get out at the right time. A *profit
is never a profit so long as it is on paper.* It must be turned
into cash. This man refused to see the market as it really
was. He was so bullish that he could not believe a 20 or
30-point reaction showed that the trend had turned, at least
temporarily. Once a man has a profit and protects it with
a stop loss order, he knows that that much money is safe
and he is sure to get it, but if he holds on and hopes, and
increases his buying at the top, he is sure to lose.

This man, after making and losing money, again went
broke in 1917, and as yet has not come back, because he is
getting too old, and he is too hopeful. To this day, he will
listen to the advice of any clerk in a broker's office or, in
fact, anyone around a brokerage office, who will tell him of
a stock that is going up 100 points, and he will believe it.
Why? Because he hopes to get in again on a stock that will
go up 100 points or more, pyramid it and make a fortune.
If you tell him that you know of a stock that is sure to go
up 5 or 10 points, he will pay no attention to you. He is not
interested in making 5 or 10 points. He wants to make 100.

Some people never learn by experience. This man has
been trading ever since before the Civil war, and in over
50 years has not learned that abnormal markets, where prices
advance over 50 to 100 points in a few months, occur only
three or four times in a lifetime. He is expecting things to
happen every year which experience should have taught him
are not likely to happen more than once in 20 years. He

does not see that markets are normal most of the time, and fluctuate in a normal way. Therefore he does not reason right or do any sound thinking. He works on an exaggerated bump of hope, and of course, meets with disappointments and losses.

You must always learn that normal profits must be accepted in normal markets, and in abnormal times you can try for abnormal profits, but protect your trades whether they show profits or not, with stop loss orders, and *be ready to change your mind* when conditions change.

CHAPTER X

CHARTS AND THEIR USE

WHAT YOU SHOULD KNOW ABOUT A STOCK

It is all well enough to know the history of a company, whether it is old or new, its earnings over a long period of years, how long it has paid dividends and its future prospects; also whether it is over-capitalized or whether the capitalization is conservative or not. But all of the information that affects the future price of the stock is contained in its fluctuations and you need nothing more than its record of prices.

A lot of people say that charts are of no value in determining the future; that they simply represent past history. That is correct; they are records of the past, but the future is nothing but a repetition of the past. Every business man goes on the past record of business in determining how to buy goods for the future. He can only judge by comparison with past records. We look up the record of a man, and if his past has been good, we judge that his future will be good.

Charts are simply a picture, which show plainer than we can convey in words. The same thing could be told in words, but you grasp it quicker when you see it in chart form. You would recognize a man and his good or bad qualities quicker from seeing his photograph than from reading a description of him.

I want no better authority on anything than the Bible. "The thing that hath been, it is that which shall be; and that which is done, is that which shall be done; and there is no new thing under the sun." This shows that history is but a repetition of the past and that charts are the only guide

51

we have of what stocks have done and by which we may determine what they will do.

If a machine instead of a human being made the market, then it might be different, but to those of us who know how to read the signs of what the manipulators are doing and of what they intend to do, charts and past records are of great value.

Therefore, you should have a chart of monthly high and low prices as far back as you can get them; then a chart of weekly high and low prices anywhere from 6 to 12 months back, and last a chart of daily high and low prices 30 to 60 days back. This will show you what the tape tells about the past, present and future condition of the stock. If the indications are not clear, you will have to wait a little while until the tape shows which way the balance of power lies and whether supply or demand is equal or one is overbalancing.

VOLUME

Do not overlook the volume of sales, for this is what tells whether supply or demand is strong enough to move the stock up or down. Consider the daily, weekly, and monthly volume of sales according to the total amount of stock outstanding. For instance:

If you look up U. S. Steel for the last three months of 1922, you will find that it was in a narrow range for several weeks and the total sales only 300,000 shares. You can not expect any big movement will take place either way immediately. Why? Because there are five million shares of U. S. Steel and one million or more shares must change hands before any big move will take place from any resistance level. The greater the volume of stock the longer the time required to accumulate or distribute a line sufficient to cause a long swing move up or down.

WHAT VOLUME TELLS

The volumes of sales on each individual stock show the percentage that is being bought and sold. That is why the tape and fluctuations tell the truth, provided you interpret

the tape correctly. Certainly a stock cannot be distributed
or accumulated without a large volume of sales. Some one
must buy and sell a large per cent of the capital stock near
bottom or top in order to cause a big move in either direction.
Therefore, study volume closely, the time required to sell a
large amount of stock, the number of points which it moves
up or down while the volume of sales is accumulating.

Suppose U. S. Steel has advanced 20 or 30 points, and
it reaches a level where there are 200,000 shares in one day,
but the stock only gains one point. The next day there are
200,000 shares and it makes no gain. This is plain enough
that at this point the supply of stock exceeds the demand, or
at least that buyers are able to get all the stock they want
without bidding prices up. In a case of this kind, the wise
thing to do is to sell out, watch and wait. If all the stock
at this level is absorbed after a reasonable length of time,
and it moves up to new high prices, it will then, of course,
indicate still higher.

In a big bull market, when stocks reach the distributing
zone, they will fluctuate over a wide range and the volume
of sales will run several times the total outstanding capital
stock. For instance: In the latter part of 1919 and spring
of 1920, Baldwin Loco. sales ran from 300,000 to 500,000
shares per week, while the stock was fluctuating between 130
and 156. This was when distribution was taking place, and
the public was full of hope and buying regardless of price.

After that, a long decline started and Baldwin reacted
to 62 3/8 during the week ending June 25, 1921. It was down
93 points from the high of 1919. During the last week of
the decline, it went down from 70 to 62 3/8, over seven points,
and the total sales for the week were less than 110,000,
which showed that liquidation had about run its course and
that there was very little stock pressing for sale. The amount
of sales at this time in one week were about half of the
capital stock and probably about as much as the floating
supply, while when the stock was nearly 100 points higher,
the capital stock was changing hands about twice each week.

After Baldwin reached the low level of 62 3/8 in June,
1921, notice it began to rally on small volume, which showed
that there was not much stock for sale and that it did not

require heavy buying to put it up. The supply of stock in the hands of the public having passed into strong hands, it was easy to start the advance in this stock which continued until it reached 142 in October, 1922, where distribution again took place. This is how volume shows you when accumulation or distribution is taking place.

CHAPTER XI

THE SEVEN ZONES OF ACTIVITY

The stock market can be divided into seven Zones which determine the different stages of activity. There are three Zones above normal and three below.

The *Normal Zone* represents something near actual intrinsic value, as far as human judgment can be depended upon and as far as the ticker tape can analyze it from supply and demand. The line marked "normal" we consider as a place where buying and selling is about equal and fluctuations are very narrow, there being no incentive or reason apparent for any wild speculation up or down. Either accumulation or distribution may take place around the Normal Zone. Investment stocks or gilt-edge bonds may start downward from this zone, while speculative issues, which have prospects or exaggerated hopes of big earnings, may start up from this zone.

The *First Zone above Normal* marks the period of quiet advancing prices which attracts very little attention. This zone may last one month, three months, six months or a year, according to the cycle the market is passing through in general conditions, because from Normal to the Third Zone at one time may be reached in twelve months and at another time may not be reached for five or ten years, viewing the market from a long swing standpoint.

The *Second Zone above Normal* marks a period of greater activity when pools begin marking up stocks. You will hear reports of better business and the public will become interested in the market and buy on a small scale, but most people will wait for a reaction back to Zone I to buy. Of course, this reaction seldom ever comes.

The *Third Zone or highest above Normal* marks a period of distribution. In this zone great activity takes place and extremely wide fluctuations. Stocks are very feverish; the public buy madly; reports of big earnings come in; dividends are increased and stock dividends declared. Everything is optimistic. Prominent men talk of the greatest prosperity ever known. Weeks and months go by and stocks continue to advance. Reactions are very small. People who wait for reactions become discouraged and buy at the market at any price. You hear of fortunes being made by the office boys, the bootblack, bookkeepers, stenographers. Everybody is rolling in wealth and all of them are dreaming of fortunes yet to be made. Most of the fortunes that they are counting on, of course, is paper profits. They have not yet cashed in, and not 10 per cent of them ever do cash in at this stage of the game. They get too full of hope to sell. This stage of the market occurred from August until the end of October, 1919. Many of my readers know what happened to them.

In this stage, for weeks and months, every few days stocks will open up anywhere from 1 to 5 points higher and keep on going up without much reaction. After this has happened and the end is near, although no one can see it, traders all go home some night, hopeful with the sky clear and not a sign of disturbing cloud, and come down next morning and find stocks opening off anywhere from 1 to 5 points. There may be no news out or any reason at all for the decline, but the real cause of it is that the market has reached the stage where Supply exceeds Demand. Everybody has bought to full capacity and there not being any large amount of buying orders in at the opening to support prices, they open off. This is your first sign of the end. Take warning! Get from under, for with this first lightning strike, you may know that the storm is gathering, and it behooves you to protect yourself. After this first sign of the end, stocks may go lower for a while and then rally up near the high points and hold for a time, but it is the warning that the "saturation point" is about reached, and the wise man will get out in time.

The history of the world shows that there never has been a time when there was a great demand for anything, whether it be a product of the mine, factory, or farm, that sooner or

later, a supply in excess of that demand did not develop.
Just as soon as any business becomes profitable enough for
a few men to make big money, enough people will get into
it to cause overproduction and force prices down. This is
but a natural law. It is caused by the weakness of human
flesh and it applies to the stock market the same as to any
other business. When stock prices reach this third zone
above normal, fluctuations are so wide and rapid that fortunes or big profits can be made very quickly. This attracts
all classes of people to the market. They buy and continue
to buy, and prices continue to rise until somebody from the
inside, outside, top side or bottom side, supplies the demand,
and the whole crowd find themselves at the saturation point
loaded with stocks, looking for a buyer, and he is not there.
Then follows the deluge back to Normal and on down to
the final and third stage below normal.

The *First Zone below Normal* is marked by a quiet
decline from high prices and what might be termed the first
bad shake-out of the weak holders. A rally follows but
stocks become dull on the rally because the Supply is still
greater than the Demand and distribution is still going on.
A lot of people who miss the market in the third stage above
normal are wise enough to sell out in the first stage down,
and professional traders, seeing that the bull market has
terminated, go short of the market on every rally with the
result that prices begin to work lower slowly.

The *Second Zone below Normal.* -- Liquidation increases,
breaks become bigger and rallies smaller; reports of falling
off in business come to light and a more conservative spirit
underlies general conditions. People are less hopeful, become more conservative and stop buying. The result is that
the market is without much support and gradually works
lower.

The *Third and final Zone below Normal* is exactly the
opposite of the third zone above. It marks a period of
panicky conditions, extreme pessimism; investors lose confidence and start selling out. There is great excitement
throughout the country and reports of poor business;
dividends are passed or reduced and even the men who were
optimistic at the top, now begin to sound a word of caution

and hint that things may get worse before they get better. The supply of stocks seems unlimited; everybody is a seller; no one wants to buy. You hear people say that they are not worth the paper they are written on. They are talking about the same stocks that they bought 50 to 100 points higher. When this stage is reached, it is the time to cover shorts and buy stocks when nobody wants them. In this stage, it may be necessary to watch and wait for several months until you see that liquidation has been completed and that accumulation is taking place, as there is always plenty of time to buy after the quiet advance starts. Remember, it is always darkest just before dawn, and it is always brightest at noontime, just before the sun starts to recede.

CHAPTER XII

HABITS OF STOCKS

The stock market is driven by human energy, i.e., prices are made through buying and selling of human beings, and as human beings have certain habits, certainly the market or the individual stocks reveal the habits and methods of the men who make markets. You should become thoroughly acquainted with the stocks you trade in, and by studying them, you will learn their individual moves which are peculiar to themselves. This is caused, as I have explained elsewhere, by a certain group of men or pools that operate in a stock for a long number of years.

Investigate and learn all you can about the stock that you trade in before you make a trade, not afterward. Study the number of points each individual stock makes in its moves up or down. Note carefully the volume of sales on which it culminates in major or minor moves. Note whether it makes it bottoms or tops by a very fast run up or by a slow, creeping movement. Some stocks make sharp tops and bottoms, some make round tops, other make square tops, some make double tops and bottoms, some make triple tops and bottoms, while others only make the single, or sharp top and bottom. By a double or triple top I mean a stock reaching a certain level, then having a big reaction and moving up to the same high level a second or third time, and vice versa.

TOPS AND BOTTOMS-FLAT OR SHARP

Stocks are no different than human beings -- they have their peculiar habits and moves. It is just as easy to tell what a stock will do by getting acquainted with it and watching its moves over a long period of time, as it is to tell what a human being will do under certain conditions after you have known him for many years. Remember that stock market movements are made by human beings; therefore they reflect what the human mind thinks and reveal the actions, desires, hopes, wishes and aims of the men who manipulate special groups of stocks that they are interested in.

Stocks do not all move alike. Some are leaders, others are laggards; some are fast movers, some slow movers.

The stocks that lead and reach top first make what we call on a chart *flat tops* -- that is, they reach a level and remain there for several weeks or months, fluctuating up or down over a wide or narrow range according to the kind of a stock, but never getting much above the level where distribution started. These stocks, of course, are the first to lead a decline when a bear market starts.

The stocks which are late movers and start their advance after the general market is about top are rushed up fast and make what is known as a *sharp top*. They do not remain long at top levels, but decline quickly, because the general market has already turned downward, and, of course, the late mover, which is going against the trend, must naturally meet with greater selling pressure at high levels than the stock which is already down considerably from the top.

Then the question might be asked, "Where does distribution take place in stocks that make sharp tops?"

They are distributed as they run up and are also sold on the way down. After making a sharp top, they usually break back 10, 20 or 30 points and then halt. At this level most people think they are down too much to sell short and have reacted enough to be good purchases; therefore they buy them. In a case of this kind, distribution often takes place 20 or 30 points below the top in the late movers, while the stocks which lead the advance are distributed within 5 to 10 points of the top.

The leaders make the same level many times, some stocks as much as 10 or 15 times, while the late mover is more of a volcanic eruption. It shoots up to the top and never makes the same high price the second time, because when the explosive buying power is over, it recedes quickly to a level that might be termed semi-normal. It is a quick recession from high temperature.

TIME REQUIRED FOR DISTRIBUTION

The time required to distribute stocks depends upon the stock, the amount of shares outstanding, general conditions and how well the stock is known or advertised among the public.

For instance: In a market like 1919, when trading averaged two million shares per day for over sixty days, it would be easier to distribute a million shares of stock in sixty days when the public were all wild and madly bullish, buying everything in sight, than it would be to distribute them in one year's time in a normal market. When stocks reach a level where distribution is taking place, they make rapid moves up and down. There is a large volume of trading and both short selling and buying is taking place. People are attracted to the stock that makes fast moves up or down, because there are great opportunities for making money.

People once convinced about a thing remain convinced for a long time. For example: A stock moves from 120 to 150 seven or eight different times -- that is, every time it comes down around 120 it rushes up again to 140 and 150. The public finally become convinced that every time it gets down around 120 it is a sure buy for quick profits. Now, eventually, after the stock has been thoroughly distributed, it declines to 120 and fails to rally. Everybody is long of it, holding on and hoping. It goes down 10, 30, 40, or 50 points, until investors and traders become disgusted, scared and sell out.

Some of the surest signs of distribution are fast moves up and down on large volume, increased dividends, stock dividends and special privileges to stockholders, which really is the bait that catches the sucker and in the end causes a big loss.

MISJUDGING THE TIME OF ACCUMULATION OR DISTRIBUTION

It requires different lengths of time in various stages of the market to accumulate or distribute stocks. A pool may

form in the early part of the year and buy a large amount
of stock, expecting a spring rise. The advance comes in
April or May, and the pool sells out, distributing its line of
stock to the public. A break occurs in June or July and the
public gets scared and sells out the stocks they bought at the
top. Then this same pool, or another one, buys back the
stocks, and another advance comes. This may go on for
three or four different times with the stock being distributed
at the different stages, which are only minor periods of distribution, and finally when the extreme high or final zone of
distribution is reached and everybody is so bullish, the stock
is distributed for a long bear campaign.

The same occurs on the way down. The market halts
and holds at one level for some time, then rallies, where the
bears put out a line of shorts and the stock continues downward, going through two or three different stages of liquidation before the final stage is reached where accumulation
takes place for another big bull campaign. This is all fully
shown on the Charts Nos. 11 and 12, showing the different
tops and bottoms on the Averages of the railroad and industrial stocks.

Bull or bear markets all move in sections of three to
four waves up or down, individual stocks working out their
high or low points according to their Time factor and individual vibrations. See chart on Industrial Alcohol which
shows the different levels or sections on the way down. Each
resistance level might have been considered a bottom, but it
was only a temporary bottom, as it shows plainly that it
failed to make higher tops on each succeeding rally.

Many stocks will halt near the end of a bull or bear campaign and make a level which looks like accumulation or
distribution, and appears to be the final top or bottom, but
if the public buy heavily, or shorts all cover around a level
of this kind, there may be built up, even at a very high or
very low level, a weak long or short interest which will cause
a final drive making the final top or bottom, as the case
may be.

Often when stocks are nearing final top, professional
shorts will put out a big line of short stocks; then something
will occur to cause them to get scared and start to cover,

and their buying, together with public buying, will force prices to a level a little higher than previous tops, all of which is plainly shown on the charts Nos. 11 and 12 on Rails and Industrials. This rule is also fully explained in the example given in regard to Retail Stores and its bottom of December, 1920, and the next bottom February and March, 1921.

RESISTANCE LEVELS

Before you start trading in any stock, get a chart on it for several years back, if you can. Study it closely. Note the levels at which bottoms and tops have been made. Find out where its previous resistance points have been made. Then you will be able to determine whether you are entering the market at a safe or dangerous level.

Suppose in 1921 you wished to buy a railroad stock which paid a good dividend and had prospects of advancement. We will presume that you made up a chart on New York Central from 1896 to date. (See Chart No. 5.) Now read about New York Central under chapter "How to Tell the Stocks that are in the Strongest Position." Thus you will see that by having a record of stocks, you get acquainted with their movements and are able to know whether you are buying near the top or bottom of a move.

Suppose you make up a chart of a stock and find that it has advanced from $10 a share to $50 and is selling at $40. This would not be a safe place to buy, because it is too close to the high price and too far away from the low price. Of course, this does not mean that many stocks which have reacted from $50 to $40 are not good purchases. I am merely giving you an example of a place of safety in buying or selling. No matter whether it is a small move or a large move, before you buy or sell you should wait until the stock shows that it is meeting with resistance one way or the other. Always remember that you should *have a reason for making a trade. Do not buy or sell on hope;* that is pure gambling and *gamblers always lose* sooner or later.

WHEN TO BUY OR SELL AFTER EXTREME TOPS OR BOTTOMS

The way to tell when to buy or sell after stocks are away from extreme tops or bottoms is to watch reactions and rallies. The average stock reacts 5 to 7 points, sometimes 10; low priced stocks 2 to 3 points.

Watch the time required to complete major or minor moves. In very active markets stocks will seldom react more than two days or the third day they will sell higher. Buy on the second day's reaction and stop three points.

If stocks get dull or narrow near bottom or top, wait for activity, then buy or sell.

After a stock has held below a top or bottom for two weeks or more, gets active and makes a new high or low, then buy or sell as soon as it gets active in new territory.

GETTING IN WHEN THE MOVE STARTS

Many people see a stock start advancing and wait for a reaction on which to buy. The reaction does not come and they get left. Reactions, cross-currents and reverse moves take place during the accumulation stage. When this is completed and the stock moves up out of the accumulation zone, it does not react much. Why? Because the insiders have bought all of the stock that they want and their next *objective point* is to move it up to the *distributing level* where they can start to sell. They do not come back to let you or anyone else get on once the move starts.

He who hesitates in Wall Street is lost. Therefore when you see a stock starting to move, if it is very active and the volume of sales large, do not wait; buy at the market.

The same rule applies to selling. When once a stock breaks out of the distribution zone, if you are long of it, sell out at the market and go short. There is no use holding on and hoping. The stock is not going to move back to a high level just to let you sell out, no more than the 20th Century train will back up to the Grand Central station to let one passenger get on after it is twenty miles out. You must get on when they holler "All Aboard" or you are left, and this certainly applies to the stock market.

Of course, you must study the stocks and be able to determine when these big moves start. As a rule, when accumulation or distribution is finished and the move is under way, you can make more money in one to two months' time, while the run is on, than you can trading for the narrow swings in six months' time.

NARROW FLUCTUATIONS AND DULLNESS

Markets nearly always culminate at the top of Bull movements with wide fluctuations and large volumes of sales, which may keep up over several months, finally culminating with several days of two to three million shares. When these signs come, take warning, for the end is near.

Bear markets, which are very rapid and fast, also wind up with wide fluctuations and large volumes of sales. For instance: On December 22, 1920, stocks declined rapidly and the volume of sales reached 3,000,000, which was the largest day of the year. The market had been declining for several weeks and the volume of sales had been running high. This was the final culmination, from which a big rally started, and many stocks have never sold lower than they sold on that date.

For many years when sales of two to three million have occurred at top or bottom, it has always marked the turning point one way or the other. When a stock or group of stocks on Averages remains for a long time in a narrow range and the volume of sales is small, it is a sign that either distribution or accumulation has run its course and the market is getting ready to turn. After short weeks, months, or years, watch which way the market turns and go with it.

Averages. -- The range on Railroad stocks in 1921 was only 11 points on Averages. The market was down to 66 on Averages against a high price of 138 in 1906. This was the shortest year's fluctuations since 1912 and indicated that liquidation had run its course, because Railroad stocks became very dead and inactive and everybody afraid to trade in them. Then the upward move started.

In comparing the position of Railroad stocks with Industrial stocks, note on Chart No. 1 of Yearly Averages that

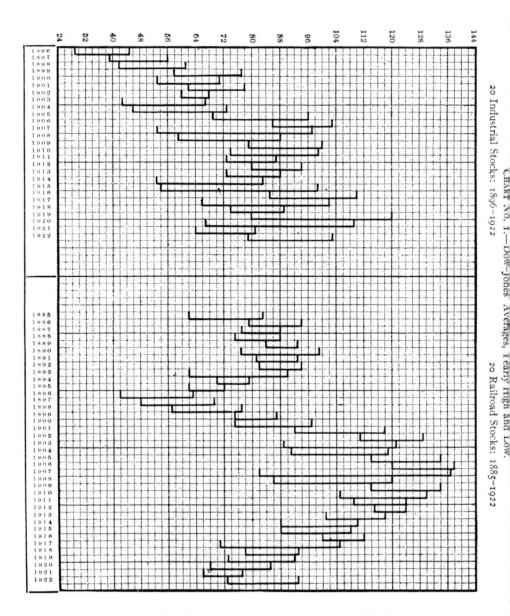

CHART No. I.—Dow-Jones Averages, Yearly High and Low.

20 Industrial Stocks: 1896-1922

20 Railroad Stocks: 1885-1922

66

both Rails and Industrials made extreme low prices in 1896; that Industrials made a higher bottom in 1903 and a still higher bottom in the panic of 1907, and declined to the same level in the 1914 depression; in 1917 made a still higher level and in 1921 went only two points lower than the low of 1917, while Railroad stocks declined below the level of every year, except 1898.

This shows that Industrials were receiving better support and were in position to advance faster than Rails. They have advanced 40 points on Averages from the low point of 1921, while Rails have advanced only 27 points. This is the way to compare the Averages of different groups or individual stocks to determine the ones that are in the weakest or strongest position.

Many stocks when they reach low levels and accumulation is taking place remain in a very narrow range for many months, but once they break out of this range, great activity develops and you should watch the trend and go with it. For example:

Mexican Pete. -- In 1918 advanced to 98 in February; reacted to 90. Traded between 98 and 90 until May, 1918; then advanced to 102. Reacted to 91 ; advanced to 102 again in June; then reacted to 96; advanced to 103 in July; then in the month of August traded in a range from 100 to 102, only two points, which was the shortest month of fluctuations in its history. This short month of extreme dullness at the top of an advance showed that accumulation was taking place and that the insiders were simply waiting, giving everybody an opportunity to sell all the stock they would and to encourage a big short interest before starting the big advance.

Therefore, this showed that it was getting ready for a big move one way or the other. In September it reacted to 98, then advanced to 104, which was above all previous tops since January, 1917. The advance continued, with only small reactions, until the stock reached 194 in October, 1918. It reacted to 146 and continued to make higher bottoms until it finally reached 264 in October, 1919.

CHAPTER XIII

DIFFERENT CLASSES OF STOCKS

DOES IT PAY TO BUY NEW STOCKS?

When companies are first organized and their stocks are listed on the Curb or New York Stock Exchange, they are held by the insiders or people who form the companies and sell stocks in order to carry on the business. Therefore, they are distributed to the public. While they may advance for a short time after they are first brought out, the man who buys and holds them is sure to have big losses, if not suffer the loss of his entire capital before he sees a profit. For example:

U. S. Steel. -- In 1901 when the U. S. Steel Corporation was organized, the common stock, of which there was 5,000,-000 shares, was put on the market around 40. It advanced to 55 and in less than 60 days, on May 9th, when the Northern Pacific corner occurred, it declined to 24. The highest it ever rallied after that was 48. It then slowly declined until it reached 8 5/8 in the Spring of 1904. The stock traded between 10 and 12 per share for nearly a year. This was the time to buy because it showed that it had reached a level where the insiders were supporting it and taking back all the stock that they had sold in the 40's.

The stock did not get above 50 until 1908. Therefore, the people who bought when it was first issued and held it had to wait seven years before they were even on it. Besides, over 75 per cent of their capital was wiped out when the stock was near the bottom, and it takes a man with a lot of nerve and a big bump of hope to hold a stock when it is that much against him. This is one of the few stocks that did come back and go higher after it was first distributed to the public. Hundreds of others are either assessed or go out of existence.

Transcontinental Oil. -- One more example of a stock
that cost the public millions of dollars in 1919. Transcontinental Oil, which was placed on the market around 45 in
1919, advanced to 62 in November of that year. Hundreds
of people were induced to buy and were told that it would
go to 100 or higher. It started on its long decline because
the insiders had sold out to the public and there was no
support to the stock. In a little over twelve months, or in
December, 1920, it sold at 6, which would wipe out 90 per
cent of the capital if a man bought it outright anywhere near
the top.

Make up a chart on this stock and study it. See how
it looks at the top and how it looks at the bottom. After
it sold at 6 in 1920, it advanced to 13 in April, 1921; then
declined to 6 in August, 1921, the stock becoming very inactive, which showed that it had reached a level where the
selling was over, and somebody was buying it. It advanced
to 12 in December, 1921, which was one point lower than
the high price of April. Then declined again to 7 1/2 in
March, 1922, where it again became inactive and dull, showing that there was support and that the stock was thoroughly
liquidated. This was the time to buy. The stock has since
advanced to 20 in May, 1922, and still shows upward trend.

Transcontinental Oil was not the exception. Almost
every other new company which placed stock on the market
in the boom of 1919 declined in the same way. Always bear
in mind that new securities are floated in boom times when
everybody wants to buy and they are put out at high prices
so that they can be sold all the way down. Therefore, great
caution should be used in buying new stocks and you should
get out quickly when they start to decline and go short.

Then, when you think stocks have reached bottom, wait
and give them plenty of time to show whether the Demand
is strong enough to give them permanent support or whether
they have reached temporary bottom, only to break out and
go lower a few months later. When stocks reach top or
bottom you do not have to be in a great hurry to get in or
out, as the insiders require a lot of time to accumulate all
of the stocks they want near the bottom and require time
to make a market to distribute them near the top.

BUYING OLD OR SEASONED STOCKS

It takes time, sometimes several years, to distribute a
large amount of stock and get it into the hands of investors
who will hold and not sell out when it advances or declines.
Therefore, the average stock is manipulated over a wide
range for many years, varying anywhere from five to ten
years, until investors absorb it all. After that if it is a fairly
good company with established earnings, it will fluctuate over
a narrow range, because the investors have it and there is no
manipulation in it.

But remember one thing, that after a stock is in the hands
of investors there is no more money in it for the insiders
until such a time as they can start a scare and get investors
to sell out. This requires a long time, because investors who
have confidence in a stock and who have held it for several
years are slow to let go of it. As long as it pays dividends
they feel safe and hold on.

Finally when it reaches lower levels than it has been for
a long time, heavier selling starts, and as there is no support
of any consequence, the stock declines rapidly until it reaches
a level where the wise manipulators are willing to buy it back
again. This is why it is often safer to sell a stock short when
it is down 50 points from the top than when it is only down
10, as all support has been withdrawn; everybody wants to
sell and no one wants to buy. I can cite you hundreds of
examples of this kind. A few will suffice.

New Haven. -- This railroad had paid dividends of 4 to
10 per cent for about thirty years. The stock was in the
hands of investors and it started to decline. When it was
down from 280 to 200 it still paid dividends. Investors held
on because they thought it was all right. Later when it was
selling at 150 in 1911 it was still paying 8 per cent and investors were holding it because they felt that it was safe; it
had paid dividends so long.

But the insiders who were out of it and had been selling
it short for many years, knew that the time was coming when
all the dividend would be passed. In 1913 the dividend was
reduced to 5 per cent and the stock declined to 66 on heavy
liquidation. The highest it ever rallied after that was 89

in 1915, the entire dividend being passed in 1914. A lot of people who had held on and hoped did not sell out when the dividend was passed, but as the stock slowly worked to lower levels they lost hope and sold the stock for what they could get, the result being that it declined to 12 in 1921.

This shows that stocks are never so low but what they can go lower and are never so high but what they can go still higher. How many people would sell New Haven short at 50 a share when they knew it had sold as high as 279? Yet, it was a safe short sale all the way down to 12. When conditions change the price at which a stock has sold makes no difference and you must play it as it is.

Union Pacific. -- The same thing applies to selling stocks short. A lot of people knowing that Union Pacific sold at 3 1/2 a share in 1896 and was assessed at $20 per share could not realize that it could be worth 50 per share in 1899. Therefore, they sold it short and went broke. In ten years after it was assessed, it sold at 195 3/8 and paid 10 per cent dividends. It went to 219 in 1909.

Therefore, people who could not forget the low prices at which the stock had sold and were not broad enough to see the changed conditions brought about by E. H. Harriman, lost fortunes bucking the trend and selling it short whereas if they had only gone with the trend instead of against it, they could have made a fortune.

Am. Sugar Refining. -- This was another stock which fluctuated wildly for many years until the stock was distributed and nearly all held by investors. Then it quieted down and remained in a narrow range for many years. In 1919 its dividend was increased to 10 per cent, the highest paid for twenty years. Yet, in the big boom and extreme high prices for sugar, the stock failed to advance anywhere near the high prices at which it sold in 1898 to 1906, the years when it was being manipulated and distributed.

In 1921 the entire dividend was passed and the stock declined to 47 5/8. Of course, everybody knows how quickly the bottom fell out of the sugar market without warning, but you might ask how the investor would know when to sell out the stock to protect his investment. We will assume that there was no indication or warning for him to sell out in 1919 at high prices. But there must be some place when a stock starts down where it will reach a level that shows weakness and support withdrawn.

In 1914, which was a panic year, the low price was 97; in 1915 low 99 1/2; in 1916 low 104; 1917, another panic year, low 89 1/8 ; 1918 low 98; 1919 low 111 1/4. Notice that from 1914 to 1919 the stock was being supported around 97 and that in 1919 the low point was 111 1/4. Now, in 1920, when the stock sold early in the year at 142, everything might have looked all right for it, but when it broke through 111, the point at which it was supported in 1919, and then declined below 98, the support in 1918, it certainly was warning enough that support had been withdrawn and that an investor should sell out. He certainly had an opportunity to buy it back again over 50 points lower if he wanted to.

Therefore, you see that you must be careful about buying stocks when they are first listed and new, and must also be careful about buying them after they have passed into the hands of investors and have become stale after the company is many years old. The time to make money trading for fluctuations, or points of profit, is when stocks are in the distributing stage, which lasts anywhere from one to five years, sometimes longer. After that you must look for new and more active stocks.

Market movements are made by men and they represent the activity and energy of human beings. A young boy is more active, moves faster than an old man, but he makes more mistakes, has more ups and downs. An old man when once he starts down hill and old age gets a grip on him, seldom ever rallies or comes up again. It is the same with old stocks. Therefore, always play the favorites, the leading active stocks which have wide ranges of fluctuations and are traded in in large volume on the New York Stock Exchange.

SELLING LOW-PRICED STOCKS SHORT

Always remember that every time somebody buys, someone else sells, and vice versa. Do not forget this fact -- that there is just as much stock when prices are low as when they are high, and somebody always owns the existing capital stock of a company. For example:

U.S. Steel. -- When Steel sold at the lowest price in its history, 8 5/8 in May, 1904, there were five million shares. Again, when it sold at the highest price in its history, 136 5/8, in May, 1917, there were still five million shares. Somebody owned the five million shares when prices were the lowest, and somebody owned the five million shares when they were at the highest. It was the insiders who owned the stock at the bottom, and the outsiders who bought it at the top, because it was paying 17 per cent dividend. While it was paying no dividend, it sold at the lowest.

A large percentage of the public buy low-priced stocks for the reason that they think they will go down less and hope that because they are low, they can go up high. This, of course, is a false impression and not based on any sound fundamental principle. Most of the time, when stocks sell at low prices, they are not worth any more, probably less than they are selling for. When they sell at high prices they are worth what they are selling for or there is some reason or cause for the high level of quoted value.

Certain low-priced stocks always become favorites of the public and they buy them, which enables the pools and insiders to sell them out. Then, of course, they go down, because there is no support. The public having bought to capacity, can not buy any more. Prices decline, and finally the public, becoming disgusted, sell out near the bottom. You can always make big profits by selling short low-priced stocks that are favorites and in which there is a big long interest. For example:

Southern Railway. -- Was a great favorite with traders throughout the South from 1901 to 1920. Every time this stock advanced above 30, they would become very bullish, hoping and expecting that it would advance to 50 or higher. A chart of it will show you that it was a good short sale every time the public bought it heavily.

Erie is another stock that the public have always bought on hope and there have often been big opportunities for selling it short at comparatively low levels, as it has always declined until the public became disgusted and sold near the bottom.

The percentage of declines in low-priced stocks is often greater than the declines in high-priced issues. Therefore, the medium low-priced stocks are safer short sales because they rally less.

BUYING HIGH-PRICED STOCKS

When a stock starts to advance, say from around 100, which is its normal level, it will meet with a lot of selling every five to ten points up because people who think it is high enough and have profits, sell out. If it continues to advance, most all of the public will sell out. Then, the professionals and the public will decide that it is too high and start to sell short. They all look for a reaction, but it does not come. The stock continues to advance until it reaches a level where all the shorts have been so badly licked that they cover up and quit.

A lot of people after seeing a stock advance from 100 to 200 become convinced that it is never going to stop going up and they buy. The result is that at a high level a weak, long interest is built up, and the short interest run in, and, of course, the stock eventually starts on a long decline. Often people who believe a stock too high at 110 will think it cheap enough at 180, after it has reacted from 200. You can always make money buying high-priced stocks when everybody is getting out because they think they are high enough for a reaction.

This is why stocks halt and react at low levels and then when they get to high levels, rush up fast and react very little, because the stock has been absorbed and the selling pressure is no longer encountered. Of course, all stock must eventually reach a level where distribution will take place, and supply exceed demand, as the only object of any one buying stocks is to sell them again. The *big money is made in the last stage of a bull market* when prices are feverishly active, and the *big profits on the short side are made in the last stage of a bear market when everybody wants to sell and nobody wants to buy.*

STOCKS THAT ARE YOUR ENEMIES

Any trader who has followed the market for ten years
or more and has been an active trader, if he will carefully
analyze his trading, will find that there were certain stocks
which he was never able to make any profits in. He always
seemed to get in too soon or too late. No matter if he sold
them short or bought them he always ended up with a loss,
while other stocks always seemed to favor him, so much so
that he would call them his pets. Now there must be some
cause for this, as nothing just happens. Everything is the
result of a cause. When you find that a stock does not seem
to work well for you, leave it alone. Quit trading in it, and
stick to the ones that favor you. I could explain to you the
cause for this, but it is not necessary, and many of you would
not believe it.

My own experience in trading and my analysis of the
cause of effects enabled me to discover the reason for these
things. For many years Mex Pete was one of my particular
pets. I could always make money in it. My forecasts on
it were so accurate that people all over the country who
subscribed to my market letter called me the "Mex Pete
Specialist." I was able to catch its moves up and down over
90 per cent of the time just the same as if I had been making
the fluctuations myself. Many other stocks work just as well
as this for me, while others do not favor me and I have never
made any money out of them. It makes no difference whether
you know or do not know the reason why a thing works or
does not work; just as soon as experience teaches you that
there is something that works against you, the only thing to
do is to quit.

CHAPTER XIV

HOW TO READ THE TAPE CORRECTLY

The best way to read the tape correctly is to stay away from it. Get the records of the day's prices and the volume of sales, make up your chart and judge it when you are not influenced by rumors, gossip or reports or by the way the tape looks when it is making a move that only lasts thirty minutes or one hour. When final tops or bottoms are made, for a major or minor move, it will be plainly shown by the volume of sales and the time consumed at bottom or top before the move starts.

A stock, in order to go up, must have reactions, but each succeeding bottom or top must be higher if the stock is going to continue upward, until it reaches a level where the selling is so strong and the volume of stock offered so great that there is not enough demand to absorb it. Then a reaction will take place and the stock decline to a level where the demand again exceeds the supply and the trend will turn up.

Studebaker. -- Notice the weekly Chart No. 2 on Studebaker which runs from September, 1920 to January 6, 1923. A decline started from 66 on September 25, 1920 and declined to 54 on October 2; then rallied to 59 in the week of October 9. For four weeks following this date, it made the same level of prices, failing to advance higher. This showed that the supply of stock was greater than the demand. A decline started on November 3 and by November 8 prices had broken below 54, the bottom made on October 2, which showed that the trend was again down.

During the period from October 9 to November 6, when prices were fluctuating within the range of two or three points, and each week getting up around 59, the man watching the tape would have been fooled many times, because each time it made 59 it would look like it was going higher,

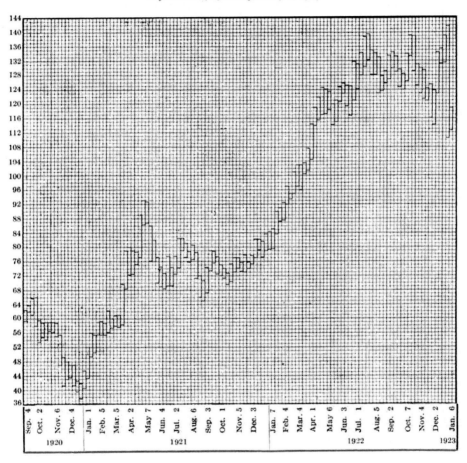

CHART No. 2.—Studebaker, Weekly High and Low.
September 4, 1920 to January 6, 1923

and how could he tell but what the buying would be great enough to carry it through. The proper thing to do when a stock makes a level like this is to sell out and go short with a stop one to two points above the level; then wait until supply or demand forces it higher or lower.

In this case, the stock declined rapidly to 41 on November 20, then rallied to 48 the following week. After that each week made a lower top and a lower bottom. In the week ending December 25, 1920, the high of the stock was 41 3/4 and the low 37 3/4. The volume was large, but the stock did not decline over two points below the previous week and it closed near the top prices of the week, which was an indication that the buying was better than the selling. The following week it advanced to 45 1/2 which was higher than the two previous weeks, but resistance was met at 47 to 48. During the week ending January 8, 1921, it advanced through this level up to 52 and continued on up to 59, the resistance levels made in October and November, 1920.

Studebaker reacted from this resistance level again back to around 55, and during the week ending February 19, advanced through this level to 62, which showed that the trend had turned up again, and if you had sold out and gone short with stop at 60, you should have covered and gone long when it crossed this level.

Note that for three weeks it held in a narrow range, but did not break back below 58. Then the advance was resumed and by April 2 it had reached 80, which was above the last high price made. From this level, the stock reacted to 72, but the following week it received support at a higher level, and so on each week until the week ending April 30, 1921, when it advanced to 93, and the volume of sales was 359,760 shares. Again the week ending May 7, it fluctuated from 92 1/2 to 87 with a volume of sales amounting to 227,300.

Now note that from the bottom, which was made during the week ending December 25, 1920, at 37 3/4, every rally was from a higher bottom, which showed that the buying was better than the selling and that the stock had not yet reached a level where supply was greater than demand until it advanced to 93, where the large volume of sales showed that there was enough selling to check the advance. Note that the week beginning May 9, 1921, the stock opened at 86, breaking the levels of the two previous weeks where there was large volume. This was the first indication that the trend had reversed and that you should sell out and go short.

This advance, which amounted to 55 points, lasted a little over four months, during which time the weekly chart shows that the trend never changed, but during this time, if you will go back over the tape, you will find dozens of times when you would have sold out and gone short and lost money. Why? Because a move that would run thirty minutes, three hours, or three days, down, would fool you and make you think that the trend had changed.

After the trend on Studebaker turned down, it declined sharply until it reached 70 the week of May 28, 1921. After that you will notice it held in a narrow range for three or four weeks and only declined less than 2 points lower than this level, which showed that there was some support. Then it rallied to 82 1/2 the week ending July 9. After holding around this level for several weeks, which showed that it was again meeting with heavy selling, the trend turned down again and it declined to 64 3/4 on August 25. Then followed a sharp rally to 79 on September 10, then five or six weeks of a slow decline down to 70; then six or seven weeks more of narrow trading in a range of about four points.

Finally, the week ending December 10, 1921, it crossed the levels made on September 10, but again halted around 82, the levels made on July 9 to 16. Then the advance started. The long period of time in a narrow range showed that accumulation was taking place. The advance continued, resistance levels being raised until it reached 124 1/2 on April 22, 1922. Then followed a quick decline down to 114 1/4 from which it advanced to 125 7/8, being higher than the previous level, but the stock narrowed down and the volume was small. In the week ending June 17, the stock declined to 116 5/8, again getting a higher support than the last level of 114 1/4 made on May 13, 1922.

Then increased volume and great activity started and the stock advanced to 139 3/8 on July 19, 1922, where the volume during the last two weeks amounted to 400,000 shares. Besides, the volume on the advance from 116 5/8 up to 139 3/8 amounted to 1,600,000 shares, which was nearly three times the total capital stock outstanding and probably five or six times the floating supply of stock. This showed plainly that distribution was taking place, and that the public was buying this stock and that the insiders were selling out.

A decline started and on August 12, 1922, it declined to 123, but the volume was only 110,000. The following week it fluctuated in about a four-point range with a volume of only 46,000, which showed that the selling pressure was not yet great enough to bring about a big decline. It advanced to 134 and again declined to 123 3/4 on September 30, failing to go through the level made on August 12.

After this, a rapid advance started and in the week ending October 14, 1922, it advanced to 139 3/8, the same level made on July 19. The volume of sales was 205,000 shares this week, which was an indication that selling was taking place and that you should sell out and go short with a stop loss order one or two points above the old level. The following week that volume of sales was 242,000 and the stock declined to 129, a plain indication that the selling was greater than the buying. The stock continued to work lower, but met with stubborn resistance around 123 to 122 where it held for two weeks.

Finally, in the week ending November 25, 1922, it declined rapidly to 116 and on Monday, November 27, it declined to 114 1/4, the same low level it made on the reaction May 13, 1922. Now the man who is simply standing at the ticker watching the tape would hardly remember that 114 1/4 was the low price made on May 13, therefore the last point where support was given, and from which it rallied to new high levels. But the man who had the record of the tape on a chart would certainly be watching this point. When it reached 114 1/4 large volume of sales appeared on the tape and it showed plainly that the support was there. This was the point to buy the stock protected with a stop loss order one to two points below the old resistance level of 114 1/4.

The stock rallied to 123 3/4 the week ending December 2, 1922, and the volume of sales was 240,000 shares, which

showed that the buying was better than the selling. Note
that the two previous weeks the highest point was 125 1/2.
In the week beginning December 9, the stock was very active
and the volume of trading large. A stock dividend of 25
per cent was declared, and the stock advanced to 134 1/4, the
volume of sales being 500,000 shares for that week, which
was the largest for any week since the stock sold at 37 3/4
in December, 1920. This was plain evidence that the public
was buying stock and that it was in the zone of excitement
and great activity which nearly always marks the end of a
movement up or down.

The advance continued, the stock reaching 141 3/4, a new
high level on December 27, 1922, which was just two days
before it sold ex-stock dividend. The volume of sales for
the week ending December 30 amounted to 240,000 shares.
After the stock sold ex-dividend, it declined to 110 3/8, then
rallied to 119 on January 2, 1923, which would equal 148 3/4
counting the stock dividend of 25 per cent.

The total volume of sales between May 13, 1922, and
December 30, 1922, amounted to over 7,000,000 shares.
The range of the stock was 114 1/4 to 141 3/4. Now, this is
where volume tells. Certainly when the capital stock has
changed hands fifteen or twenty times in a range of 27 points,
after this stock is up over 100 points, there is no question
but what distribution is taking place and the stock is getting
ready for a long decline. Therefore, instead of investors
buying the stock because it pays 10 per cent, and has declared
a 25 per cent stock dividend, they should sell out and go
short.

Now, the question is to determine the position of the
stock in January, 1923. After it advanced to 119, it started
to decline and short sales would be in order with a stop loss
order at 120 to 121. The resistance level at 114 having
been broken, the trend of the stock is down, and when it
breaks 110, the price made on December 29, 1922, it will
be in a weaker position and should be followed down until
signs of support, both in volume and time, are shown. By
time I mean that the stock must hold a resistance level for
several weeks without breaking lower. The period of time
required to distribute Studebaker was about eight months,

or from April to December, 1922. Note the last period of accumulation when the stock sold around 65 and fluctuated between that price and 80, that the period of accumulation was about six months, or from June to December, 1921, and that the stock advanced 76 points from the low point made on August 25, 1921, and if you count the stock dividend, it advanced about 84 points.

This same rule and reasoning should be applied to any other stock that you wish to determine the trend of. During the period of accumulation or distribution, the man who tries to read the tape must get fooled dozens of times and make mistakes in trying to follow minor moves which do not mean anything. Therefore, the correct way to read the tape is to keep up a chart showing moves of from three days to one week and the amount of volume. Of course, you must consider the total outstanding stock and the floating supply. Again I *emphasize* the *fact* that the *correct way* to *read* the *tape* and *interpret* it *accurately,* is to *stay away from it.*

CHAPTER XV

WHEN THE TAPE FINISHES AND GIVES FINAL SIGNALS

The truth that the tape has to tell you cannot be told in one day, in one week, or in one month. It begins to tell its story the first day that a stock reaches the buying or selling zone, but it requires time to complete the story; to assemble all of the facts; to finish the accumulation or distribution and give the final signal that a new move is on. Chart No. 3, showing U. S. Rubber at the top of 1919, is an important and valuable example of this.

U. S. Rubber. -- When U. S. Rubber advanced to 138 in June, 1919, and reacted back to 124, then rallied to around 138 again, holding until August around the same level, it showed that selling pressure was sufficient to stop it. It declined to 111 in September; rallied again to 138 in October, made 139 in November; declined to 113 in November, receiving support 2 points higher than the September bottom. Then rallied to 138 in December and in January, 1920, advanced to 143, or 5 points above the high price made in June, 1919.

Now, making a new high, would ordinarily be an indication that it was going higher, but after a stock advances into new territory, if it is going higher, it will continue on up without breaking back below the old top levels. In this case, U.S. Rubber, within a few days, declined to 136 which showed that heavy selling had been encountered; that the new high level was made at the expense of shorts and outside buying; that the selling which started in June, 1919 was still there and that someone was supplying the stock.

A rapid decline followed in February, 1920, and when the stock broke below 112, which was under the last support point, it was a signal that distribution had been completed

83

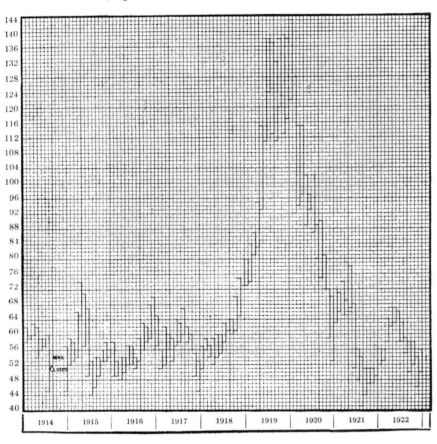

and that a big downward move would take place. In the previous June, 1919, after U. S. Rubber had advanced from 45 in December, 1917, it showed that it had reached a level where heavy selling had commenced, but the tape could not tell when this selling would be completed, and all the stock distributed. But it did tell the final story in February, 1920, when it broke under 112 and promptly declined to 92, and never rallied above 115 again until it sold at 41 in August, 1921. All the way down the selling pressure was plainly indicated, and the stock continued to make lower tops and lower bottoms. The tape was telling part of its story all the time, but it did not show that it had finished until November, 1921, when, after three months in a narrow range, the stock moved up into new high territory.

Thus you see that after any big advance or big decline, it requires time to tell when the next big move is going to start, and the man who expects to read this from the tape, day by day, will get fooled many times. Therefore, he should wait until he gets a definite indication before deciding that the big trend has turned and a major move started. The larger the capital stock of the Company, or the more shares outstanding, the longer it requires to complete accumulation or distribution. The length of time, as well as the total number of points that a stock has moved up or down from high or low levels, must be considered in judging whether accumulation or distribution is taking place.

After U. S. Rubber was up 100 points from the low and had reacted from the same high level for eight months and after the panicky decline in November, 1919, had plainly shown that the bull market was over, you would not expect that U. S. Rubber making a new high, was going to very much higher levels. But you should wait a few days to see whether the price could be maintained before going short. The daily high and low, weekly high and low chart and the total volume of sales will help you to determine when a false move of this kind is made, and the trend reverses, because a move of this kind into new high territory, causes all the shorts to cover and leaves the stock in a weak technical position.

TIME FOR ACCUMULATION AND DISTRIBUTION

When a stock uses up several months' time either in accumulation or distribution, it will require then several months for the run between accumulation and distribution. All of the stock is not sold on the first rally, nor even on the second or third. Stock has to be bought and the market supported on the way up until it reaches a level where the supply is greater than the demand and the insiders are willing to sell out. Then it hesitates and moves up and down over a narrow or wide range, according to the kind of stock, until distribution is completed.

The same occurs when a stock starts down. It requires a long time to convince people that after a stock has been selling at 140, it is going down 100 points. Some people buy when it is down 10 points, others buy on 30, 40 and 50-point reactions, believing the stock cheap because they remember the price at which it formerly sold -- 140, with the result that when it continues downward, they all get scared and sell out, causing the last rapid decline which may be anywhere from 10 to 30 points.

If people would only learn to watch and wait, they could make a lot more money, but they are in too big a hurry to get rich, and the result is they go broke. They buy or sell on hope, without a reason.

BOOK III

HOW TO DETERMINE THE POSITION OF STOCKS

"Read, not to contradict and confute, nor to believe and take for granted, nor to find talk and discourse; but to weigh and consider."

-- FRANCIS BACON.

A man has to buy and sell to make a profit, that is, he has to get in right and get out right. Then he must watch for the proper time to start his trade and the proper time to close it. Getting in right does not help if you fail to get out right. The time to act either when buying or selling must be determined by the condition of the market at the time and by the position of the individual stocks that you intend to trade in. You might be able to buy and make profits in some stocks after a bull campaign has about finished, while others you might be able to sell short and make profits after the major swing of a bear market has finished. This is fully explained under the chapters "How to Tell the Stocks in Strongest Position" and "How to Tell When Stocks Are in Weak Position."

Do not buy a stock of one group just because some stock in another group goes up. Neither sell a stock of the same group because some one of that group has already started down. Analyze the position of the stock you intend to trade in. Find out if it has passed out of the accumulation or distribution zone. Stop to think before you act; look before you leap; examine before you buy and remember that it is always better to be safe than sorry. It is much better to take a small loss quickly than to hold on and hope and take a big one later.

CHAPTER XVI

POSITION OF GROUPS OF STOCKS

It is very important to watch the position of the different groups of stocks. To be a success you must keep up with the times and follow the leaders. The way to do this is to keep up a monthly high and low chart on several stocks of each different group; also keep a yearly chart of the different stocks. The further back you have records the better you will be able to judge the position of a group.

Many years ago Traction and Railroad stocks were the leaders. Then followed the Copper boom. After that the Motors, Rubbers and Oil stocks. Of course, every few years some kind of a boom develops in different mining stocks, but they are a class of stocks which you have to be very careful of, as they are probably the most uncertain of all.

During the past few years the man who stuck to Rails has made very little money because the opportunities have not been there. The Motors, Rubbers and Oils have been the stocks which have made wide fluctuations and offered unusual opportunities for trading.

The day of Railroads is passing and the big fortunes will not be made in them in future. Competition is getting keener every day in the Motor industry and it will eventually narrow down to a good return on invested money, but will not produce enormous profits. For this reason you must be wide awake and in future look to the new things which will offer unusual opportunities and attract speculators, causing wide fluctuations.

In future you must watch for the new industries that develop and get into their stocks, just the same as the people who let Rails alone and got into motors and made a fortune. Those who sold out Coppers in 1916 and played the Oils in 1918 and 1919 made fortunes.

In my judgment, the Aeroplane and Radio stocks will
be the ones in the next few years that will make fortunes
as great as any that have been made in Oils or Motors. The
Chemical stocks also offer great opportunities in future, as
this country has made great progress along chemical lines
since the war and the business is growing on an enormous
scale.

A wide range is what the trader requires in order to
make big profits. As long as stocks move between 20 to 100
points each year, you certainly will be able to make some
money on the long or short side, probably both. But when
they narrow down to 5 and 10 points in a year, your chances
are very much against big profits.

In 1916 Copper stocks reached the highest level that
they had made for many years. But in 1919 when Oils and
Industrial stocks reached the highest level in their history,
Coppers only had a moderate rally. After that they worked
lower each year until 1920 and 1921. By keeping a chart
of this group and some of the leading issues, you would be
able to see that in 1919 the Copper stocks had been heavily
distributed because they failed to rally to the 1916 level.
Therefore, they were good short sales for a long decline.

CHAPTER XVII

GENERAL TREND OF THE MARKET

There is always a certain group of stocks which will follow the general trend up or down, while others for a long time will work opposite to the general trend. The Dow-Jones 20 Rails and 20 Industrials for many years past have been the best guide for the main swings, but since the number of stocks listed on the N. Y. Stock Exchange have increased from 100 to over 700, naturally there must be a large number of stocks which will follow their individual trend and not the general trend of the market. Therefore, it is necessary to make a close study of the individual stocks and determine their trend regardless of the trend of the general market.

An example of this kind occurred in the decline in October and November, 1922. When all of the active leaders like Baldwin, Crucible Steel, Studebaker, and U. S. Steel were declining rapidly, Continental Can was advancing almost every day. Look at Chart No. 4 on Continental Can and see the different position it was in as compared to Baldwin Locomotive and other stocks. It had made a new high level and showed plainly that its trend was up, which it would follow regardless of the trend of the general market. I have explained this in regard to stocks that are late movers and those that finish before and after final accumulation or distribution is completed.

While you could have been selling Baldwin Locomotive, Crucible Steel and other leading stocks and making big profits in the decline of November, 1922, at the same time you could have been making big profits by buying Continental Can. Many traders foolishly sold Continental Can because it looked high, was advancing and paid no dividend. This was in direct violation of my rule to always sell the weak

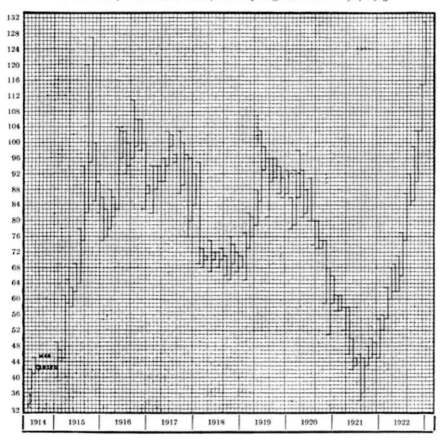

stocks and buy the strong ones, which is really following the trend of each individual stock. By watching closely the daily high and low, weekly and monthly charts, you will be able to determine when each individual stock has changed its position from strong to weak.

CHAPTER XVIII

HOW TO TELL THE STOCKS IN STRONGEST POSITION

If you are waiting for an indication to buy stocks, you want to select the strongest stock in a certain group, as the stock which is in the strongest position is naturally the one that will lead in a Bull market and the one in weakest position will lead in a Bear market.

STUDEBAKER

Suppose in 1920 or 1921 you were watching and waiting to buy one of the Motor stocks. Note that the low price on Studebaker in 1917 was 34; again in 1918 low 34. The high in 1919 was 152. It declined to 38 in December, 1920, holding 4 points above the support levels of 1917 and 1918, which showed that it was in a strong position. However, the general group of Motor stocks in the Spring of 1921 did not show any sure signs of having made bottom, but Studebaker led the advance.

It made 93 in April, 1921; then followed the decline in May, June, July and August, which carried all the Motor stocks to new low levels. However, Studebaker, in August, 1921, when final bottom was reached in the general list, was still selling at 65, up 27 points from the low of December, 1920, while other Motor stocks were lower than they had sold in 1920 or the early part of 1921. This was a plain indication that Studebaker was receiving strong support. Otherwise, it could not gain 27 points while others were losing.

It remained in a quiet, narrow range from 65 to 72 for several weeks, showing plainly that it was well supported and being accumulated. If you had been waiting to buy again, this would be the time. After that Studebaker worked up, making higher tops and higher bottoms each month, as shown on Chart No. 2.

On May 16, 1922, the low price of the reaction was 114 1/4; on June 12, 1922, low price 116 5/8; then on August 11, 1922, the low of the reaction was 123; again on September 29, 1922 low 123 7/8, showing progressive bottoms. On November 27, 1922, it declined to 114 1/4, the same support level of May 11 and 16, 1922, from which it rallied to 141 3/4 in December -- the highest of the year.

A 25 per cent stock dividend was declared in November, 1922, and as the stock had been placed on a 10 per cent dividend basis in July, 1922, besides an extra dividend of $1.50, it was only natural to suppose that this was the last good news which the stock had discounted. After it sold ex-stock dividend in December, 1922, it declined to 110 3/8, breaking all previous support levels and indicating that the trend had turned down. Therefore should be sold short on all rallies. It may remain in a distributing range for several months before it starts on a long decline, but at this writing shows plain enough that it is going lower.

RAILROAD STOCKS

On Chart No. 1 which shows the yearly high and low of the 20 Railroad stocks, you will notice that the extreme high price was made in 1906 and that after the 1907 panic stocks rallied in 1909 within a few points of the highest level. After that they continued to work lower. In 1916 and 1919 when Industrial stocks made the highest prices in history, as you can see by the chart, railroad stocks only made feeble rallies. In fact, after the rally in 1916 rails made lower bottoms and lower tops every year until June, 1921.

After the Average low price on Rails in June, 1921, they continued to advance, reaching 77 in December, which was the high of the year, as you can see from the chart. In January, 1922, they reacted to 73; then advanced to 78 in March, 1922, which was higher than the level of 1921 and the first time that Average prices had made a higher top on the yearly chart since 1916. In fact, in 1916 the rally was only 4 points above the 1915 high and the big trend on Railroad stocks was really down from 1909 to 1921. So when finally they made a new high, it was a sure indication that the trend had turned and that they were going higher. They advanced to 93 on Averages in October, 1922, where they met with a resistance at the same high prices of 1918 and 1919.

Now, suppose in 1921 that you knew rails must reach bottom some time and were watching to find the strongest one to buy. Refer to New York Central Chart No. 5.

N. Y. CENTRAL

It is an old stock and you can get its record for a long number of years back and see how it established zones of accumulation and distribution. In 1893 low 90; 1896 low 88; 1907 low 89; 1908 low 90 1/8. This shows strong support between 88 and 90, and that the stock had been bought around these levels in panicky depressions over a period of 15 years.

In 1914 it broke 88 and declined to 77. Now, after breaking the support of such a long number of years, it was a plain indication that the stock was going lower and that it should be sold short and that you should watch for a new base of support before buying again.

In 1917 Railroad Stocks declined below the panic price of 1914 and 1907. In fact, the Averages reached the lowest they had been for nearly twenty years. The Government was forced to take over the Railroads in order to handle business on account of the war.

In December, 1917, New York Central made a low of 63. In February, 1920 low 65; in June, 1921 it again sold at 65, showing that for four years it had received support at the same levels. Yet, during 1920 and 1921 Southern Pacific, Great Northern Pfd., Northern Pacific, Norfolk & Western, Missouri Pacific, Wabash Pfd. A and many other railroad stocks had sold lower than they had for many years. New York Central held up although the Averages of Rails were several points lower than the panic price of

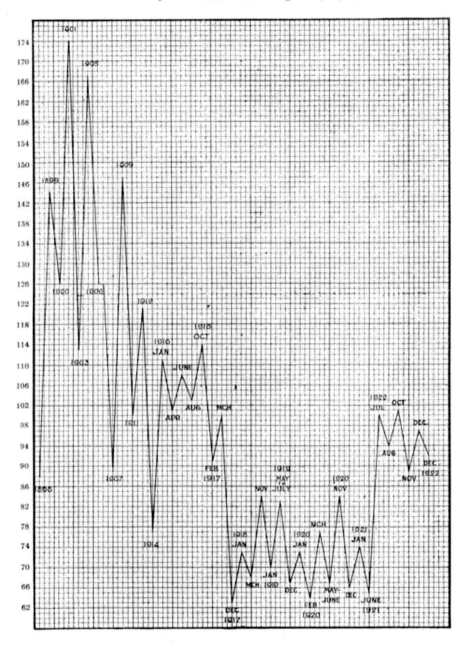

1917. This was another opportunity to buy with a stop 3
points under the old base of 63.

The high price made between 1917 and 1921 was 84.
After being accumulated between 65 and 75, the stock
crossed 84 in March, 1922. This was a signal for much
higher prices, and if you wanted to pyramid, should buy
more at this level. It advanced to 101 in October, 1922,
where distribution started, and then began making lower
bottoms, showing that the trend had turned down.

St. Paul. -- Another rail that made lower prices every
year from 1909 until 1921. It has shown accumulation for
some time and at this writing both the common and preferred
stocks now indicate that they are on the upward trend.

Rock Island. -- Made a low price of 16 in December,
1917, and has been making higher prices each year. Note
how it led the advance in 1922 and made a new high. This
is the way to select the stocks to buy. The ones that will
not go down, and make higher bottoms in years of depression,
will certainly lead the advance when the turn comes.

Southern Railway. -- Another stock that is now in a very
strong position. Has made higher bottoms ever since 1913
and still indicates higher prices.

Union Pacific. -- Low in the panic of 1907 was 100; in
1917 low 102. Another stock that you had a chance to buy
at the old support level. February, 1920 low 110; June,
1921 low 111, a still higher support, and the place to buy
with a stop loss order under 110.

You can see that Union Pacific made higher supports on
each big decline from 1907 to 1921, while numbers of other
railroad stocks were reaching new low levels all of these
years, which showed that they were in a weak position and
without much support. Union Pacific rallied to 154 in September, 1922, where distribution started.

BUYING AND SELLING POINTS

You follow this same rule in any group of stocks in order
to locate the strongest or weakest individual stock of the
group. When you have the record of a stock for a long
number of years back and see where it gets its support in

extreme panic years and where it meets with resistance in boom years, you can easily tell the levels where it is safe to buy or sell with a risk limited to two or three points.

American Can. -- The low in July, 1914 was 20. It advanced to 68 in October, 1915; declined to 51 in 1916; then advanced to 68, the same top, where it held for several months without going higher, giving you a chance to sell out and go short. It declined to 30 in the panicky break of 1917 and advanced to 68 in September, 1919, where it held for nearly two months without advancing into new territory. This was another opportunity to sell out and go short with a stop 3 points above the old level.

It declined to 22 in December, 1920, which was two points above the support level in 1914. It rallied to 32 and again in June, 1921 declined to 24, receiving support at a higher level. Then remained for four months between 24 to 29, showing plainly that the stock was being accumulated. You could then have bought again around these levels.

In the fall of 1922 it crossed 68, the old resistance levels, which was an indication for higher prices and you should buy more.

American Loco. -- In December, 1920, low 74; rallied to 91 in May, 1921. Declined to 74 in June, 1921, receiving support at the same level and giving you an opportunity to buy with a stop under the old base. It advanced to 117 in April, 1922, which was the high price made in October, 1919. At this level you should have sold out and gone short with a stop loss order at 120, or 3 points above the top. It then declined to 109 and held for several weeks in a narrow range, failing to break the support level around 108, which was made in March and April, 1922.

In August, 1922, it made 118, crossing the old levels and indicating higher prices. It advanced to 136 in October, 1922, where it met with heavy selling and the trend reversed. In November, 1922 declined to 116, which was the old resistance level of October, 1919, and April and May, 1922. A stock nearly always gets support the first time it reacts back to old high levels and the main trend would be considered up as long as it stayed above old resistance levels.

CHAPTER XIX

HOW TO TELL WHEN STOCKS ARE IN WEAK POSITION

You always want to know the stocks that are in the weakest position, because they are the safest to sell short in a Bear market. The ones that show weakness first naturally will be leaders in a Bear market. After the trend turns down from the top and stocks have declined for quite awhile, the next thing which will show that a bigger decline will take place is the breaking of important support points.

INDUSTRIAL ALCOHOL

Started up from a low price of 15 a share in January, 1915. Advanced to 170 in April, 1916; again in 1917 advanced to 171 and in May, 1919 advanced to 167. Declined to 120 in August, 1919, and made the last advance to 164 in October, 1919. Notice on Chart No. 6 that the selling zone from 167 to 171 extended over a period of four years.

Now, notice the support points. December, 1916 low 95; November, 1917 low 99; December, 1918 low 96; December, 1919 low 98. This stock showed distribution and that it was in a weak position, because in 1919 when Industrial stocks reached the highest Average in history, this stock failed to reach its previous high levels made in 1916 and 1917. Therefore, it was getting in position for a big decline.

When it broke the support of 95 to 99, it declined to 78; then rallied to 102, and continued to work lower until November, 1921. Yet, many other stocks made low prices in December, 1920 and in June and August, 1921, but Industrial Alcohol declined to 35. So you see what enormous profits can be made on the short side if you pick the stocks that are in the weakest position and continue to follow them down as long as the trend continues to show lower.

99

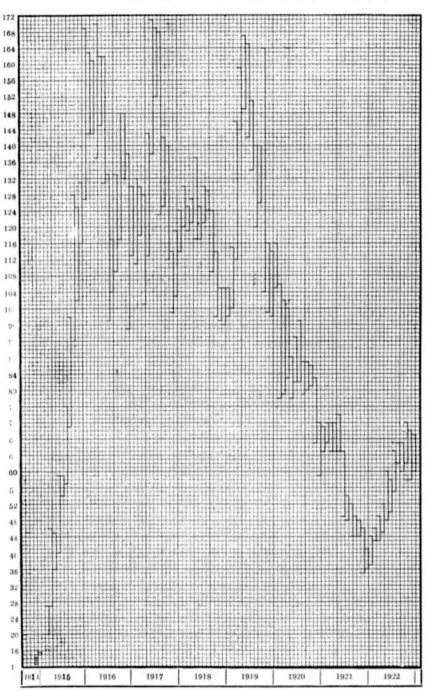

Notice how many times you could have bought the stock between 100 and 96 and how many times you could have sold it around 165 to 170, making profits every time on both the long and short sides. Then, finally when the support around 96 was broken it declined 50 points more. Again I remind you that stocks are never too low to sell as long as the trend is down, and never too high to buy as long as the trend is up.

After Industrial Alcohol reached 35 it remained for about two months in a 5 or 6 point range and since that time has been making higher tops and higher bottoms. It reached 72 in October, 1922, and as this stock was one of the last to make low prices in 1921, it will naturally be one of the last to complete its upward swing.

If you had been short of this stock in June or August, 1921, when other stocks made bottom, there would have been no reason for covering as it was making lower prices every month and showing plainly that the trend was down. You should at least have waited to cover until it made a higher price than a previous month, which would have been 42, when it went over the high price of December, 1921.

ATLANTIC GULF AND WEST INDIES

Another stock which had a phenomenal rise in the Bull campaign of 1919. Notice that its support levels in 1917 and 1918 were between 88 and 92. You could have bought it around these levels numbers of times and sold it out with profits of 15 to 20 points. It had a top, or resistance level from 1917 until the early part of 1919 between 117 to 120, where you could always have sold it and gone short. It declined to 92 in February, 1919. The previous low price was 89 made in December, 1917. This was the place to buy, protected with a stop under the old support levels.

It advanced and in April, 1919 crossed 120, which was an indication for much higher prices. In May, 1919 it crossed the high of its history, 147; advanced to 188 in June; reacted to 140 in August; advanced to 192 in October, 1919.

After that it began making lower bottoms and lower tops. In February, 1920 it declined to 137; rallied to 176 in April, 1920, where it again was distributed for several months, finally breaking the support of 137 and continuing the decline, the rallies getting smaller all the time.

In November, 1920 it broke through the supports at 92 and 88, which left no other support level except the low price of 27 made in 1916. It declined to 62 in December, 1920, and while other stocks were rallying in January, 1921, it continued on down, finally declining to 18 in June, 1921.

After making bottom for two months at 19 it started to rally. Advanced to 36 in December, 1921; reacted to 24 in February, 1922, holding for several weeks at this higher support point; advanced to 43 in May, 1922; then declined to 19 in January, 1923, where it was again supported, and you should buy with a stop two to three points under.

Thus, you can see how safe it is to sell a stock and keep short of it as long as it shows weakness, regardless of what other stocks are doing.

CHAPTER XX

JUDGING FINAL TOPS AND BOTTOMS

Before any stock, or group of stocks, starts on a big advance or decline, a long period of time is required for preparation, or accumulation or distribution. It requires time to prepare and lay the foundation for a building. The larger the building, the more time required to construct the foundation. It is the same with stocks. The greater the advance or the decline, the more time required in preparing for it. For example:

U. S. STEEL

Take U. S. Steel which was incorporated February, 1901. It was a new stock and the largest corporation of its kind in the world at that time. Its common stock was all water, and as water seeks its level, Steel common with its five million shares of water had to seek its level. It required many years to reach that level. The stock declined from 55 in 1901 down to 8 3/8 in 1904. When it reached the level of 12 it remained from December, 1903 to September, 1904 fluctuating between 12 and 8 3/8. Most of the time the fluctuations were between 9 and 10. It was at very low ebb, slow narrow fluctuations with very small volume of sales. This is where accumulation took place, which required about ten months and gave you ample time to watch it and see that it was receiving support. You did not have to be in a hurry about buying, as it was preparing for its long advance.

We will overlook the top at 94 7/8 in 1909. However, you can look it up for yourself and see that the entire capital stock changed hands several times between 88 and 94, and some days the trading in this stock alone ran over half a million shares, which, of course, showed that it was being distributed. Now, look at the final top in November, 1916 on Chart No. 7, when it reached 129 3/4. There was a wide range of fluctuations and big volume. It declined to 101 in December, 1916, rallied to 115 in January and early February, 1917, and on February 3, 1917, when the Germans declared the U-Boat war, it declined to 99, which was only two points under the December low. Then the advance started, which carried it up to 136 5/8 in May, 1917.

The volume around this top was over fifteen million shares, or three times the total capital stock. Note the 3-point chart, which shows how active it was and how it was moving up and down while distribution was taking place. The distribution of this stock was really going on from October, 1916 until May and June, 1917. Therefore, the man who wanted to sell out and go short had plenty of time to watch the stock and determine when distribution had been completed. It was getting ready for a long decline, but had advanced 98 points from its extreme low level of 1914, and it required time to distribute it. But note after distribution was completed, how rapidly it declined, reaching 80 in December, 1917.

The general impression among the public is that "as steel goes so the market goes"; that is, they feel that U. S. Steel is the leader, either up or down. There was a time when it was the leader, but it is not now. The majority of stocks made high prices in October and November, 1916, and were at much lower levels in May, 1917; yet U. S. Steel went 7 points higher in May, 1917 than the high of November, 1916. People who bought other stocks, expecting them to follow the lead of U. S. Steel and make higher prices than in 1916, got badly fooled and lost their money. This is another illustration and proof of my rule: "Do not buy stocks of a different group because some other stock is strong."

GENERAL MOTORS AND STUDEBAKER

Trade in the stock that gives the strong or weak indication; do not try to pick one to follow it. Judge each stock according to its individual position, -- by Time, Space and Volume. Do not expect General Motors to have a big

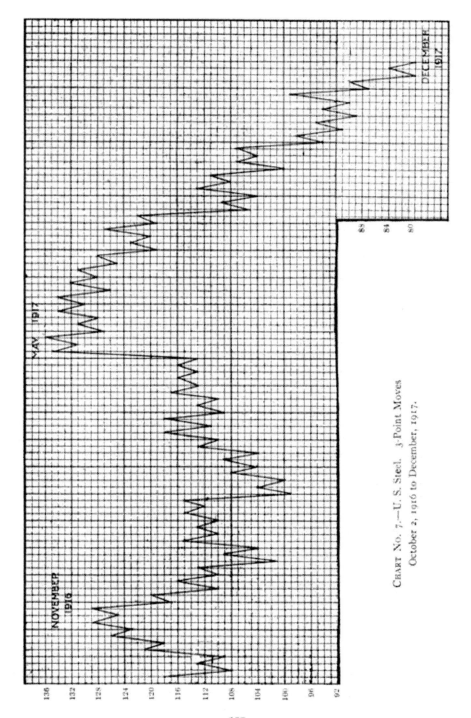

CHART No. 7.—U. S. Steel. 3-Point Moves
October 2, 1916 to December, 1917.

105

advance because Studebaker has already advanced. Look
up General Motors chart and note its position. Also consider that it has a capital stock of fifty million shares, while
Studebaker has only 750,000 shares. Don't forget it requires
buying power to put a market up and selling pressure to put
it down. It requires a much larger buying power to move
a stock with several million shares than it does one with only
750,000.

Did you ever stop to consider that with a stock like
General Motors, each point up or down means a gain or
loss of fifty million dollars on the total capital stock? This
is why so much buying and selling occurs at every point and
why it moves so slow. When General Motors increased its
stock in 1920 and issued 10 for 1, the price was 42 in March,
1920, which equalled the value of 420 per share for the old
stock. A slow decline started. It reached 13 in December,
1920, which was nearly 30 points down in nine months' time.
This big decline was produced because with fifty million
shares, there was no pool that was willing and had the money
to support it. It continued to decline until it reached the low
price of 8 in January, 1922; then advanced to 15 in June,
1922.

This advance of 7 points seemed very small compared
with what Studebaker and other motor stocks were doing.
Yet, the percentage was just as great. Studebaker advanced
from a low of 65 in 1921 to a high of 141 in 1922, which
was a little over 100 per cent increase on its selling price,
and General Motors advanced from 8 to 15, nearly 100 per
cent on its selling price. So many people get fooled in buying
low-priced stocks and simply hope and expect them to
advance in points almost proportionate to a high-priced stock.
Low-priced stocks do advance and decline in proportion to
high-priced stocks, and even greater at times, when you figure
the percentage on the price at which they are selling.

AMERICAN SMELTING AND REFINING

Note Chart No. 8 on American Smelting and Refining,
and the long period of accumulation from September, 1901
to May, 1904 when it made a range from 37 to 52. Now,

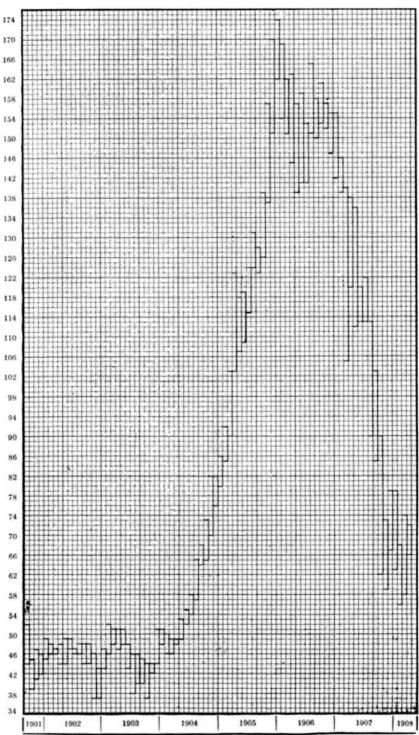

when once it broke out of this range of accumulation, it was
a plain indication that the advance would last for a long time,
and that it would be a big one. It advanced to 174, never
having any big reaction. It reached the high price in January,
1906; then distribution started which lasted for a year. It
fluctuated between 174 and 138 and finally in January, 1907,
broke under the distribution point of 138 and declined rapidly,
reaching 56 in February, 1908. Thus you see that after great
activity and a long time in a narrow or wide range at top
or bottom, a big move follows in which you can make profits
rapidly. Then how foolish it is for anyone to try to buck
the trend or to hold on and hope when stocks start to go
against them.

Suppose that when the advance in this stock started, you
sold short around 50 because it was near the old high price.
When it crossed 52, it plainly showed up, because it was in
new territory. Suppose you decided to wait for a reaction to
cover your shorts, which reaction did not come. The stock
advanced to 62, 72, 82, 92, and on up to 174. What good
would margin do? You would simply be throwing your
money away, because you would be bucking the trend. Again
let us suppose that you started selling short at 100, and tried
to average, as so many people foolishly do. You would have
been ruined.

The same thing applies to the man who bought the stock
around 138 in early 1907, and it declined to 56. What
chance would he have, trying to average or by buying the
stock outright and paying for it? He never would have
gotten out. Just go over records of stocks for as many years
back as you like and study them, and you will find out that
it does not pay to buck the trend or try to average. The
proper way to trade is to go with the trend, and pyramid
while you are making profits, and not when the market is
going against you. I reiterate: *Stop your losses quickly and
let your profits run.*

PROGRESSIVE TOPS AND BOTTOMS

It always pays to keep a chart of Averages of any group
of stocks, as you can then judge when they have reached a

level where they are receiving support or being distributed. But, of course, you cannot trade in Averages; therefore, must keep a chart of some of the individual issues of each group in order to determine the best ones to trade in and the right time to buy or sell.

On active stocks 5 to 10-point moves will help to show when tops or bottoms are being made. On stocks selling 25 to 60 per share 3-point charts will show best, but on stocks selling 100 to 300 per share 5 and 10-point moves are much better because it requires a wider range in which to buy or sell a large amount of stock.

Sometimes stocks require several years to lay a foundation for a big Bull or Bear campaign. Suppose you were keeping Oil stocks in 1913 and were watching for something which would lead an Oil boom when it developed. Take California Pete.

California Pete. -- The low in 1913 was 16; 1915 low 8; 1916 low 16; 1917 low 11, at which price it remained in a narrow range for about four months, showing that the stock was receiving support at a higher level than the low price of 1915. Having declined from 72 a share, the high price in 1912, it had shown accumulation between 16 and 8 from 1913 to 1917.

It advanced to 56 in 1919; declined to 15 in November, 1920, and advanced to 71 in July, 1922. This is what we call "progressive" bottoms, i.e., each support several years apart being higher. 1915 support 8; 1917 support 11; 1920 support 15; and in 1921 low 30. As long as a stock makes higher bottoms and higher tops, the trend is up and it is safe to follow the advance. This rule applies to daily, weekly, monthly or yearly movements.

Mexican Pete. -- Another example of progressive bottoms or higher support. In 1913 low 42; 1914 low 51; 1917 low 67; 1918 low 79. In October, 1918 made its first big advance to a new high and reached 264 in October, 1919; declined to 84 1/2 in August, 1921, making a still higher bottom than the last bottom in 1918. So you see all of these years Mexican Pete was receiving support at higher levels, which showed that it was preparing to reach extreme high levels before distribution would take place.

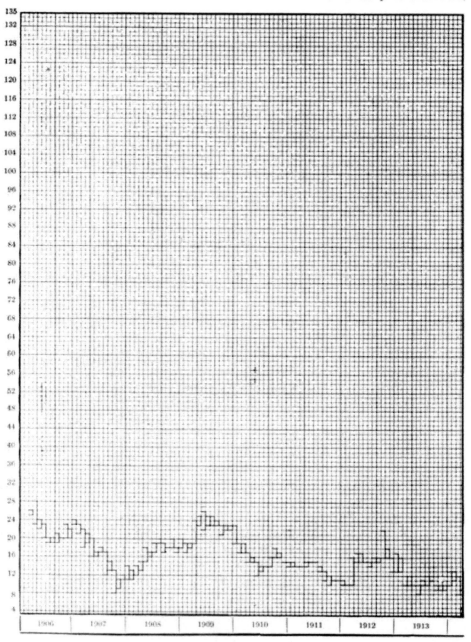

Monthly High and Low. 1906–1922

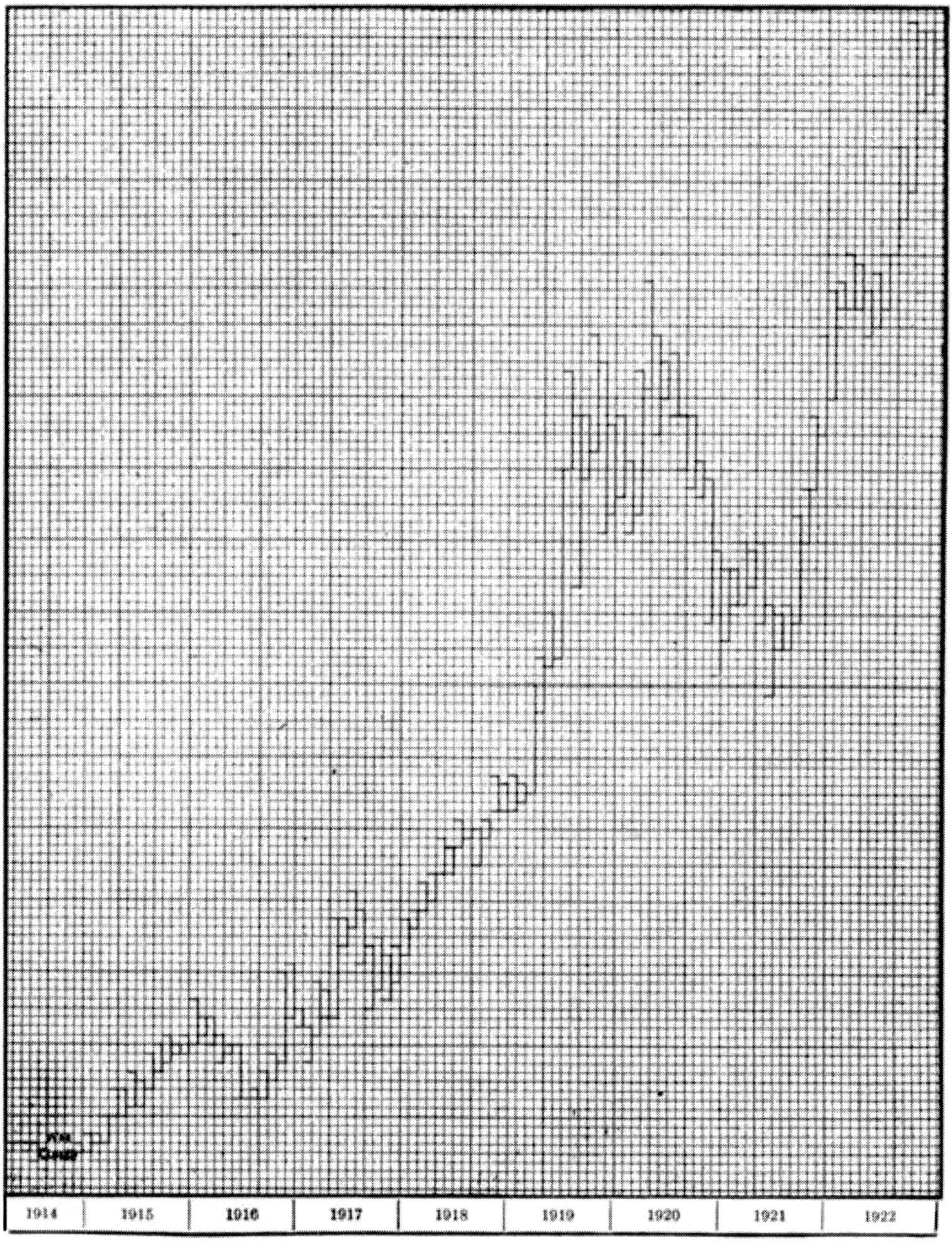

Look up in the same way any stock you are interested
in or wish to trade in and note its position over a long number
of years. The larger the accumulation or distribution and
the more time consumed at top or bottom, the greater the
advance or decline will be. As an example, -- see Chart No.
9 on Corn Products.

Corn Products. -- Sold at 28 when it was first incorporated in 1906. It declined to 8 in 1907; advanced to 26
in June, 1909; declined to 10 in 1912; advanced to 22 in
1913; declined to 8 in 1913; rallied to 13 in 1914; declined
to 7 in July, 1914. It remained in a narrow range and did
not sell above 10 until the Spring of 1915.

It was first supported at 8 in 1907; again at 8 in 1913;
and on the extreme war scare sold at 7 in 1914, and showed
a long period of accumulation. 28 had been the high of its
history, which price was made in 1906. It crossed this level
in 1917. This was a period of ten years that the stock had
ranged most of the time between 20 and 8, showing a long
period of accumulation and getting into new high territory
showed that it was in position for a big advance.

In 1919 it advanced to 99; declined to 77; then advanced
to 105. In December, 1920 declined to 61; rallied to 76 in
March, 1921; then declined to 59 in June, 1921, receiving
support two points lower than the previous level. Then it
advanced to 134 in October, 1922.

Thus, you see that after the stock crossed its high level
for ten years, it became more active than ever, never reacted
below 24 and steadily advanced to 105 in 1920, the reactions
being very small and every bottom higher and showing plain
indication of the upward trend.

It is just as important to determine where stocks reach
top or distributing zones in order to sell out and go short
as it is to find accumulation and the bottoms at which to buy.
Refer to Chart No. 3 on U. S. Rubber:

U.S. Rubber. -- Notice that it reached 138 in June, 1919;
made the same high in July; made 137 in August; again in
October made 138; in November 139, and in December,
1919 made 138. During all this time the bottoms had been
between 111 and 117. The stock was finally rushed up to
a new high of 143 in January, 1920, and quickly broke back,

which was an indication that distribution had been completed and that it was ready to start on the long decline.

It began making lower tops and lower bottoms every month, but when it broke through 111, it showed that all support had been withdrawn and that distribution had been completed. The stock declined to 41 in August, 1921. Its support points from 1914 to 1917 had been between 44 and 45.

You might ask why certain stocks reach levels over a long number of years where they meet with support or resistance. The reason is that the same men manipulate these stocks. They are usually on the inside and know something about their value. Therefore, they buy them around a certain level and hold until they reach a level which they consider high enough; then sell out and go short, or wait unti] they decline to around the same levels again, where they buy for another campaign. You should study very carefully the stock that you trade in, in order to determine what its past points of support and resistance have been.

THE SIGNS OF A CHANGE

When you see the clouds gather you know that it is a sign of rain, and you seek shelter, because experience has taught you that certain formations of clouds invariably indicate rain or storm. When you see the same signs in the stock market that have always meant distribution in the past, you should take it as your warning, stand from under, and protect yourself against the decline. Likewise, when you see the same kind of bottoms that have always indicated accumulation, you should cover shorts and buy.

You judge a tree by the fruit it bears; in stocks you must judge each by its own signs and signals and not by what other stocks do. When you get an indication and the time comes to buy or sell, place your order at the market; do not limit buying or selling prices. This often causes losses because you miss your market by an eighth or a quarter and thus lose big profits. When it is time to get in or out, never quibble over a fraction; do not lose points by trying to save an eighth.

CHAPTER XXI

NUMBER OF TIMES A STOCK FLUCTUATES OVER THE SAME RANGE

Very active stocks and those that are high priced, when they reach a level where the insiders want to unload, make rapid moves up and down for several months over a wide range, which causes traders to buy and sell because there are unusual opportunities. The stock remains around the high level long enough for them to become accustomed to the price and feel safe enough to buy.

Suppose that a stock has advanced 20 or 30 points straight up, without much reaction, and it reaches top. It can not be distributed in one day, one week, or one month, but the sure sign of accumulation or distribution is a stock moving up or down many times over the same range, especially making moves of 5 points or more without getting above its high point, and at the same time not breaking under its resistance levels on the down side. Sometimes a stock will move over the same range anywhere from 10 to 20 times, working up and down.

Note Studebaker in 1922, and Industrial Alcohol, U. S. Rubber, and American Woolen in 1919. You will see how they fluctuated up and down over a wide range while distribution was taking place. Studebaker moved up and down over the same range over 20 times between 114 and 139 between May and November, 1922. The big swings up and down over this same range were only 5 or 6 times, but counting 5-point moves or more, it covered the same territory over 20 times. That showed that distribution was taking place, and that it was preparing for a long move down.

WHEN TO STAY OUT AND WATCH

If you have been successful and followed a bull campaign up for many months and accumulated a big line of profits, you must be on your guard for the first real indication of a change in trend and the end of the bull campaign. When you get this sign of the end, which, as I have explained, is larger volume and rapid, feverish fluctuations, then get out, watch and wait; that is, sell out your long stocks and wait for the opportunity to go short. *Never be in a hurry to get in again once you are out with a good profit.* Opportunities always come again in the stock market if you only have the patience to wait for them.

Another time when you should get out and watch is after the first signs are shown that a bear market is culminating. It takes time to accumulate stocks and you do not want to get in too soon. If you have made big profits on the way down, you can afford to wait a few weeks or months until the signs are plain that another bull market is starting.

INSIDE INFORMATION

Wide fluctuations occur more often at high levels than at low levels, because distribution is taking place. When stocks reach very low levels after a final drive, they slow down and often work for some time in a very narrow range while accumulation is taking place. Accumulation and distribution are exactly opposite. When the insiders want to sell stocks, they make all the noise possible and do everything to attract the attention of the public and create a large public buying power. When stocks decline to low levels and they want to accumulate a large line, they work just as quietly as possible. They use every means to disguise the fact that they are buying stocks, and do everything to discourage the outsiders from buying them.

There is nothing wrong in the tactics employed by manipulators. It is simply business policy, and you would pursue the same policy if you were in the same position. They must buy stocks from some one, and they want to buy them as cheap as they can. Then you cannot expect the fellow on the inside, if he is honest and working for his own interest, to tell you that he is buying. Neither can you expect, when stocks get near the top and he is selling, that he will tell you that he is selling out, because he thinks they are high enough. He would be a fool if he did, because in order to cash in and get his profits, he must sell stocks to some one.

So many people believe the only way to make money in the stock market is by getting "inside information." I can tell you, after twenty years' experience, that inside information is impossible, and the sooner you get the idea out of your head that inside information will help you, the better off you will be. If you were playing poker with a man, would you expect him to show you his hand, and not expect to see yours? He certainly would not, and you know that he would not. If he did, you would win all his money. Then, why do you expect the man on the inside, whether he be a banker, pool manager, manipulator, investor or otherwise, to tell you what he is doing when he is trying to make a market to sell out a line of stocks or to accumulate a line?

You may be able to find out what he is doing if you can interpret the tape correctly, because it tells the story of everybody's buying and selling, and it never lies if you know how to read it right, for neither the insiders nor the outsiders can hide or disguise the amount of buying or selling. Every share bought or sold is registered on the tape. If you know how to correctly analyze the volume of sales and space movements, you will be able to tell when to buy and sell.

The most important thing of all is the *Time* factor, which I use in making up my annual forecasts. It is not my object here to give away that secret, but I am showing you plain enough and giving you rules enough that, if you follow them, you will be able to make a success in the stock market. The price you pay for this book means nothing. One idea that I give you may be worth thousands of dollars to you in the next five to ten years' time, if you will only follow it. If I only succeed in teaching you how to avoid losing your money for the first three to five years, and you can keep even and get experience, then there is no estimating the value of this knowledge, for after a few years' experience and study, you will then be able to make money rapidly.

CHAPTER XXII

CROSSING OLD LEVELS

When stocks establish certain levels of accumulation or distribution over a long number of months or years and then cross them it is almost a sure sign that they are going to new high or low levels before they meet with resistance again. As a rule it is always safe to buy or sell a stock around old bottoms or tops with a stop loss order three points above or below previous high or low prices. For example: see Chart No. 10 on Republic Steel.

Republic Steel. -- In 1916 the high was 93; 1917 high 94; 1918 high 96. It was a sale every time it reached these levels. In 1919 it crossed 96 and advanced to 104; then reacted to 81; crossed 96 the second time and advanced to 145. A stock going into new high territory the second time is always safer to buy than the first time, as the first time it goes through it is likely to meet with a lot of selling to drive it back, but the second time the stock has all been absorbed and it is easy for it to advance. Note from 1914 to 1919 the bottoms were "progressive" or higher on Republic Steel.

Wabash Pfd. A. -- December, 1916 high 60. Worked lower each year, making lower bottoms and lower tops until December, 1920, when it reached 17. It ranged between 18 and 24 all during 1921, while accumulation was taking place. Declined to 20 in August, 1921, making another higher bottom, and sold at 20 every month from August, 1921 to February, 1922. Here was a strong indication of support and you should buy the stock with stop at 18, and buy more when it crossed the high price of 24 made in 1921. It advanced to 34 in April, 1922, which was the old resistance level of October, 1920. Distribution took place and it declined to 23 in December, 1922, receiving support and remaining in a 2-point range for several weeks; then started upward again.

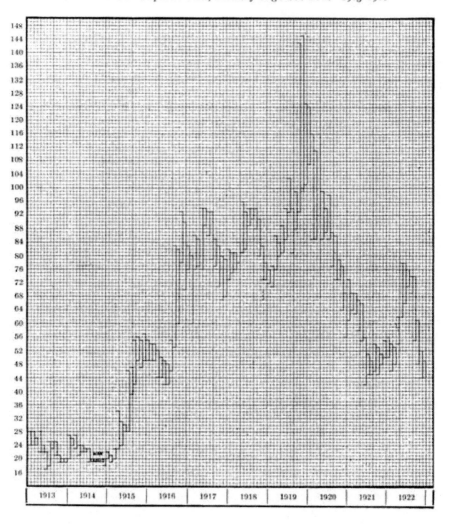

In studying the different groups of stocks, you should watch the position of each individual stock to see which one is in position to lead an advance or decline.

Crucible Steel. -- Started its big advance in 1915 and made 109 7/8. It made lower tops in 1916, 1917 and 1918. The bottom in 1916 was 51; in 1917 low 46; 1918 low 52. When the stock crossed the high price of 1918, it was an indication for a further advance, and when in 1919 it had crossed the top of its history, 109 7/8 made in 1915, it was a sure indication that it was going to make extreme high prices.

The fact that it held around 46 to 52 for three different years on declines showed accumulation. Crucible advanced to 278 in 1920, which, of course, was an extreme price and not based on intrinsic value. Therefore, after doubling the capital it suffered an extreme decline back to 49 in August, 1921, where it was again in its old zone of bottoms and was a purchase for another advance.

CUTTING AND INCREASING DIVIDENDS

I have stated before that you should never sell stocks just because they do not pay dividends, nor buy them because they do. In December, 1921, Crucible advanced to 69. It was then paying 4 per cent. It declined to 53 on February 27, 1922. Early in March the dividend was passed, when the stock was selling around 58. It declined to 53 1/2 and failed to break the low price made before the dividend was passed. This was an indication that the passing of the dividend had been discounted, and that if the stock could hold above the levels previously established, it was a purchase regardless of dividends.

It advanced to 98 in September, 1922, which was the level from which the last break started in 1921. Around this time a new issue of stock was offered to stockholders at $100 per share. This caused selling in the old stock and reversed trend, the stock declining to 59 in November, 1922.

Always watch a stock when new stock is offered at a price around which the old stock is selling. If the old stock fails to get higher than the price at which the new stock is offered,

it is an indication of good selling and you should sell out and
go short.

United Retail. -- Another instance of the effect of dividend reduction is United Retail Stores. The low price made
in December, 1920 was 46. The stock rallied to 62 in May,
1921; declined to 47 in August, 1921, again receiving higher
support. It advanced to 57 in January, 1922 and showed
every evidence of having been accumulated for the past year.
In February, 1922, when the stock was selling around 53,
the dividend was cut and it declined to 44.

Now, if you had bought around the old level of 1920 --
46 -- and placed a stop 3 points away, or at 43, it would
never have been caught. During March, 1922 the low was
44 and the high 47, a 3-point range for a month, which
showed that the stock was being supported. It opened at
45 in April; then the advance started. Suppose you had
waited until it crossed the high price made in March and
bought at 48. In a little over thirty days after that time,
the stock advanced to 71. After reacting 10 points, continued on up to 87 in October, 1922, the old resistance level
of 1920, where it met with heavy selling, and declined to
66 in December, 1922, another resistance level.

This shows you that the insiders knew a long time before
the dividend was cut that it was going to be cut, and they
were buying the stock. Now, all you had to do was to wait
and see if they would give it support around the previous
low level. After they had held it for two months without
permitting it to break 3 points under the old bottom, it certainly was safe enough for you to buy and risk 3 points on.

In many instances when dividends are cut it is the time
to buy as the worst is known and has been discounted. As
a rule when dividends are increased and extra dividends paid,
the insiders are distributing stock and they bring out the good
news in order to entice the public into buying. I could cite
you hundreds of instances, but one example will suffice.

U.S. Steel. -- Advanced to 136 5/8, the high of its history,
in May, 1917. It was paying 5 per cent dividend. The
dividend was then increased, or an extra dividend paid, which
equalled 17 per cent. But the stock never sold as high again
and declined to 70 1/4 in 1921, because the insiders knew that

the earnings were the best they probably would ever be and it was the time to bring out the good news and facilitate distribution of the stock.

Book Values. -- Another thing I wish to call your attention to that misleads many an investor is "book values." Statisticians had figured the book value of U. S. Steel at around $250 a share in 1917, and, of course, the poor suckers who bought it at the top thought it would go there. As far as the advance in price is concerned, "book values" mean nothing, because the company is not going to be liquidated. Therefore the book value is only good to create false hopes and make people buy and hold on, thinking that the stock should sell somewhere near its book value. Not one stock in a hundred ever sells anywhere near the book value.

In February, 1915, U. S. Steel passed its dividend. The stock was selling around 40. It declined to 38 and has never sold lower since. That was the time to buy a real bargain, not when it paid 17 per cent and sold above 130.

In 1915 the high on U. S. Steel was 89; in January, 1916 low 80; again March and April, 1916 low 80. The stock held in a range of 9 points for nine months and in August, 1916 advanced to 90, which was above the high price of the previous year. After holding for so long in a narrow range, it was a sure indication of a big advance, because the stock had been accumulated. Otherwise, it would have declined below 80. It advanced to 129 without reacting five points.

After the high price of 136 5/8 in May, 1917 it declined to 80, the low price made in 1916, where it received support. According to the rule, you would have bought with a stop 3 points away, or at 77. It advanced to 116 in August, 1918. Remained two months around 116, which showed that distribution was taking place and that you should sell out and go short with a stop 2 or 3 points above 116. It declined to 89 in January and February, 1919; remained for two months in a very narrow range without breaking the bottom of the previous month. Here was another chance to buy with a stop 2 or 3 points under the old bottom.

The stock advanced to 115 in July, 1919, failing by one point to reach the 1918 top. Here you should sell out and go short again with a stop above the old levels. The stock continued on the down trend and in 1920 broke the bottom of 89 made in 1919 and also broke the support points at 80 made in 1916 and 1917, which showed that support had been withdrawn and that it was going lower. It declined to 70 1/4 in June, 1921. Remained in a narrow range during July and August, fluctuating between 72 and 76. This showed that accumulation was taking place and that you should buy with a stop loss order under 70, or buy as soon as the stock crossed the levels made for two months, which showed that the trend had again turned up.

It advanced to 111 in October, 1922, where it reached the distributing zone of 1919 and 1920. At this writing it shows that distribution is taking place and the stock is getting ready for another downward move before the end of 1923.

You should always study each individual stock separately and learn how to follow its moves. No two work just exactly alike; neither do all stocks make tops and bottoms at the same time, but they do show plainly when they are in a strong or a weak position, and you will be able to judge the position of a stock in each different group by making up a monthly high and low chart for several years back.

WHEN STOCKS MAKE NEW HIGHS OR LOWS

When a stock advances or declines into new territory or to prices which it has not reached for months or years, it shows that the force or driving power is working in that direction. It is the same principle as any other force which has been restrained and breaks out. Water may be held back by a dam, but if it breaks through the dam, you would know that it would continue downward until it reached another dam, or some obstruction or resistance which would stop it. Therefore, it is very important to watch old levels of stocks. The longer the time that elapses between the breaking into new territory, the greater the move you can expect, because the accumulative energy over a long period naturally will produce a larger movement than if it only accumulated during a short period of time.

1921 HIGH PRICES

1921 was low year of the depression. Although there
was a strong rally up to May, 1921, most stocks made low
prices in June and August, 1921. Now just look up a list
of stocks and see the ones that crossed the high prices made
in the early part of 1921. They are the ones that led the
1922 bull market and had the biggest advances, while stocks
that failed to make the highs of 1921 are yet selling at low
levels (January, 1923). Following are some examples of
stocks that made new highs:

Allis Chalmers: 1921 high 39; advanced to 59 in 1922.
American Can: 1921 high 32; advanced to 76 in 1922. When it crossed 68
    it was in new territory for its history and indicated much higher prices.
    Up to this writing in 1923 it has advanced to 84.
American Smelting: 1921 high 44; advanced to 67 in 1922.
American Woolen: 1921 high 82; advanced to 105 in 1922.
Atchison: 1920 and 1921 high 90; crossed this price in 1922 and advanced
    to 108 in September, 1922.
Baldwin: 1921 high 200; advanced to 142 in 1922.
Canadian Pacific: 1920 and 1921 high 129; crossed it in February, 1922 and
    advanced to 151 in September, 1922.
Chile Copper: 1921 high 16; 1922 high 29.
Coca Cola: 1919 high 45; 1920 high 40; 1921 high 43; crossed all of these
    highs in the early part of 1922 and advanced to 82.
Continental Can: 1919 high 103; 1920 high 98; 1922 high 68; crossed all
    of these highs and advanced to 124 in 1922.
Great Northern Pfd.: 1921 high 79; crossed in 1922 and advanced to 95.
L. & N.: 1921 high 118; crossed in 1922 and advanced to 144.
New York Central: 1921 high 76; crossed in 1922 and advanced to 101.
Pan Pete: 1921 high 79; advanced to 100 in 1922.
Sinclair Oil: 1921 high 28; advanced to 38 in 1922.
Studebaker: 1921 high 93; crossed it in January, 1922 and advanced to 141.
U.S. Cast I. P.: 1921 high 19; advanced to 39 in 1922.
U.S. Steel: 1922 high 88; advanced to 111 in 1922.

Thus you see that all of the stocks which crossed the high
of May, 1921, early in 1922 had big advances, because they
were in strong position, and the buying power being strong
enough to carry them over the previous years highs, showed
that they were going higher.

STOCKS THAT DID NOT CROSS 1921 HIGHS IN 1922

You will note that the stocks which did not show strength
in the early part of 1922, and were unable to advance any-

where near or cross 1921 highs, have proved to be laggards and are still selling at comparatively low levels (up to this writing). This again proves my rule to *buy the strong ones and sell the weak ones,* and do not let the price at which they are selling prejudice your judgment, as the stock that is selling the highest will often continue to advance while those that are selling low will continue to decline.

The following stocks failed to cross the highs of 1921 during 1922. Note the levels at which they are now selling (January, 1923):

American Agricultural Chemical: 1921 high 50; selling at 32 at the end of 1922.
American International: 1921 high 53; selling around 26 at the end of 1922.
American Linseed: 1921 high 60; selling at 32 at the end of 1922.
American Sumatra Tobacco: 1921 high 88; although this stock is a late mover
   and did not make bottom until after the other stocks, it was still selling around 28 at the end of 1922, which is near low levels.
Atlantic Gulf: May, 1921 high 44; selling at 22 at the end of 1922.
Chandler Motors: 1921 high 85; 1922 high 79; selling at 65 at the end of 1922.
International Paper: 1921 high 73; selling around 52 at the end of 1922.
Pierce Arrow Common and Preferred: High of 1921, 41 and 49 respectively; both selling at low levels at the end of 1922.
United Drug: 1921 high 105; did not rally above 84 in 1922.
U. S. Industrial Alcohol: 1921 high 74. It was a late mover and did not make bottom until November, 1921, but only rallied to 72 in 1922 and failed to cross 1921 top.
Virginia Carolina Chemical: 1921 high 42; selling at 25 at the end of 1922.
Worthington Pump: 1921 high 55; declined to a new low level -- 27 -- in November, 1922.

You see that Pierce Arrow, Chandler, and General Motors all failed to make 1921 highs and at the end of 1922 were selling at low levels, while Studebaker, which made a new high in the early part of 1922, was selling at a high level in December, 1922. General Asphalt 1921 high 78; rallied to 73 in 1922 and failing to reach the high of 1921, showed that it was meeting with heavy selling, because it remained a long time around high levels; then declined to lower prices than it made in 1921. This is the thing to watch. When stocks advance near old high levels and remain a long time and fail to go through, distribution is taking place, and as soon as they break out of the distributing zone, they should be sold short. Traders who bought Asphalt, expect-

ing it to follow Pacific Oil, Mexican and Pan Pete, suffered
big losses, because the other stocks showed that they were
in strong position, while General Asphalt showed that it was
in weak position.

The Rubber and Sugar stocks all failed to cross the high
prices of 1921, and at the end of 1922 were selling at lower
levels. The Rubber stocks have recently (January, 1923)
started to advance, and if they cross the high levels of 1921
and 1922, they will then indicate higher prices and may
continue to advance while other groups of stocks decline.
Then, you should buy Rubbers and not sell them, expecting
them to follow stocks which made high levels and were distributed during 1922.

BUYING OR SELLING AFTER A STOCK SHOWS CHANGE IN TREND

After accumulation or distribution takes place, a stock
moves into new territory, either high or low, showing that
the stock has been absorbed or distributed and that a new
move is starting.

Refer to Chart No. 9 on Corn Products. Note that
after the stock halted at 108 and remained for several weeks
in a narrow range, while it was being absorbed between 106
and 108, fluctuations were very narrow and you would not be
able to make much money trading in it. But if you bought
it after it crossed 108, which showed that the trend had
again turned up, you would have been able to make 20 points'
profit in less than 60 days.

Now, the same condition will develop in the opposite
direction. Since September, 1922, the stock has been holding
for over four months between 124 and 134 and you would
only be able to make small profits trading in and out. After
it breaks 124 it will show plainly that the trend has turned
down, and if you sell short then, you no doubt will be able
to make quick profits.

The *big profits* are made *in the runs between accumulation and distribution*. Therefore, you *make more money*
by waiting until a stock *plainly declares its trend* than by
getting in before it starts. It is just like a race. It often

takes fifteen or twenty minutes to get the horses away from the post, but once "they're off" the race is over in two minutes. It is the getting ready that takes the time, the run is soon made, once the firing line is crossed. What difference does it make whether you buy a stock 10, 20 or 30 points above the bottom so long as you make profits?

The same with selling short. It makes no difference how much the price is down from the top. When it breaks *out* of the *distributing zone,* it is a *safe short sale* and you will make *quick profits. Get the idea of prices out of your head. Forget about the bottoms and tops; trade to make profits, not to try and catch the bottom or top eighth. The insiders do not do it, and you can not hope to do better than the man who makes the market.*

CHAPTER XXIII

TOPS AND BOTTOMS ON RAILROAD STOCKS

In another chapter I have told you about stocks and groups of stocks which are leaders, and you should always follow the leaders, either up or down. From 1896 to 1909, the railroad stocks were the leaders, and banks discriminated against industrial stocks in loans and accepted the rails as gilt-edge securities.

Note on Chart No. 11 the low price of the Dow-Jones 20 Rails was 42 in August, 1896. After a long advance, they made the first important top in April, 1899, when prices reached 87, although they were within 1 to 2 points of this same level in February and March. A big reaction occurred in May, which carried prices down to 78. A rally followed in September, bringing prices up to 86, within 1 point of the April top. They met with stubborn resistance at this level, and declined to 73 in December, 1899, then rallied to 82 in April, 1900, and again in June declined to 73, making a double bottom or reaching the same price as made in December.

After this double bottom, a big advance started, which did not culminate until May, 1901, when prices reached 118. On May 9, 1901, the Northern Pacific corner took place, which caused a panicky decline, average prices declining to 103. This was the first sudden big break in the bull market and showed that it was over for the present, and that you should then watch for a rally to sell on. A rally followed in the latter part of May and in June, carrying prices near the top of May. Then a decline to 105, where prices held for four months, just above the level made in the May panic. Here accumulation took place again, while stocks were moving over a narrow range.

Then followed a long slow, advance to September, 1902,

CHART No. 11.—Dow-Jones' Averages, 20 Railroad Stocks, Monthly High and Low.
1896-1922.

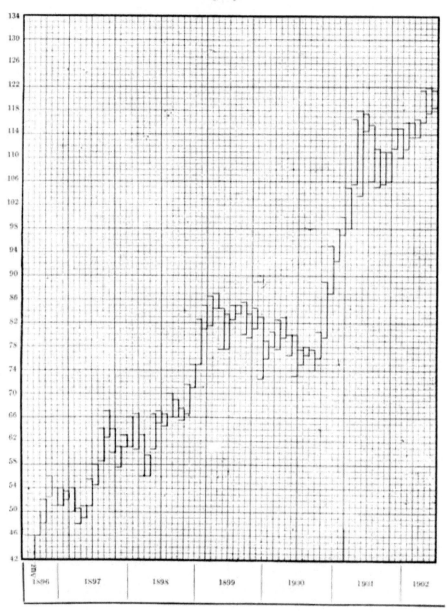

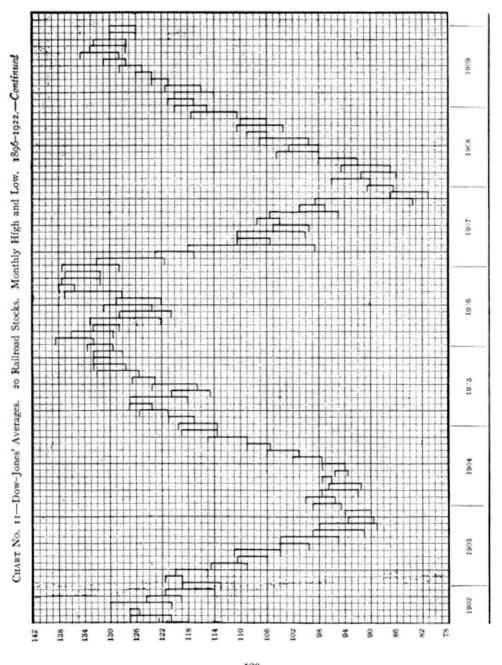

CHART No. 11—Dow-Jones' Averages. 20 Railroad Stocks. Monthly High and Low. 1896–1922.—*Continued*

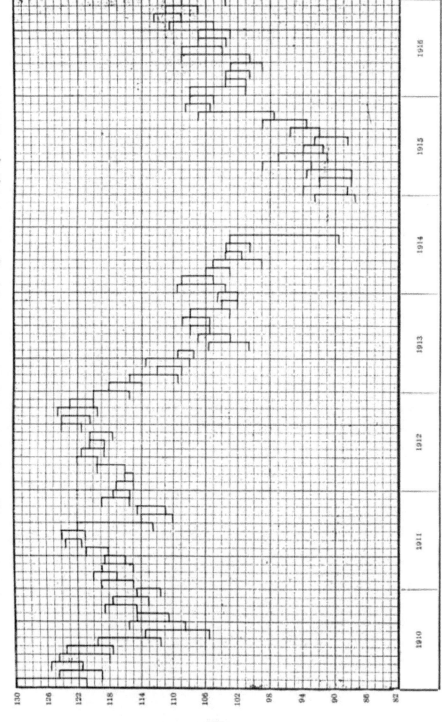

CHART No. 11—Dow-Jones' Averages. 20 Railroad Stocks. Monthly High and Low. 1896-1922—Continued.

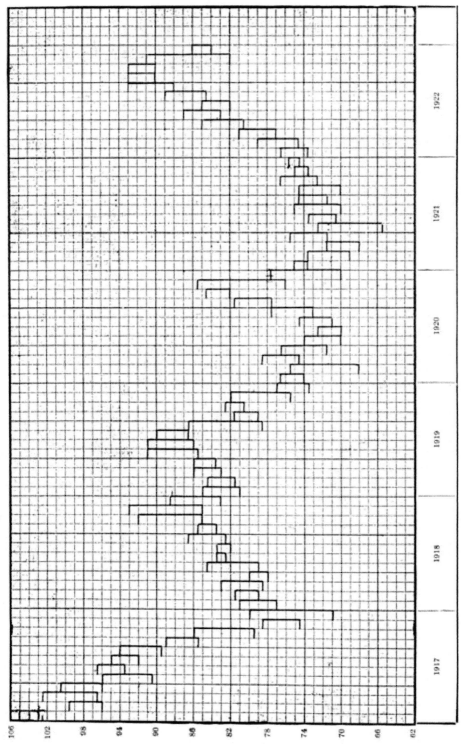

when prices reached 129, where they made a sharp top which was followed by a rapid decline to 89 in September, 1903. Note that accumulation occurred from September, 1903 to June, 1904 at which time the bull market was resumed. Stocks rallied to 127 in April, 1905, this price being within 2 points of the high level of September, 1902. A rapid decline carried prices down to 115 in June. Then they advanced to 138 in January, 1906, which was the highest in history and Averages were up 96 points in ten years. Prices started to decline and following the San Francisco earthquake, declined to 120 in May, 1906. Then they advanced to 138, in September, making the same top as in January.

They remained around this same level with fluctuations narrow, until January, 1907 when they broke out of the distributing zone, and after such a long period of advancing markets, with distribution which had lasted for over a year, it was but natural that a drastic decline should follow. A silent panic occurred on March 14, 1907, carrying prices down to 98. This was one of the most rapid declines that has ever occurred on the Stock Exchange. After this, a sharp rally followed; then another decline, bringing prices down to around the low levels of March 14, and in some cases, stocks selling lower. After this, the market rallied and held up until August, but was very dull on the rallies, which showed that liquidation had not been completed. Liquidation started again in September, 1907, and finally wound up with a panicky decline in November, when the Averages reached 82, which was 56 points down from the high of the early part of the year.

Accumulation took place until March, 1908, when the bull market started again, which culminated in October, 1909 with prices at 134, within 4 points of the highest in history. Here they met with resistance, and distribution took place over a narrow range, lasting about six months. The decline started in 1910, and wound up with a sharp break in July, which carried the Averages to 106. This was a sharp bottom, and prices rebounded quickly. They continued upward until July 1911 when the Averages reached 124. Then fluctuations became narrow at the top, and the market was very inactive for several months. A sharp decline occurred in August and September, carrying prices down to 110. Then followed a slow advance to August, 1912, when prices reached 124, the same top as 1911. Here they made a flat top from August to October, 1912. Then declined to 100 in June, 1913. The market was narrow and inactive, and slowly worked up to 110, making a slightly lower level than April, 1913. There was a small rally and a narrow market in May and June, 1914, and in the early part of July the big decline started, which wound up with a big break after the war broke out and caused the Stock Exchange to close on July 30th.

The Exchange opened again on December 15, 1914, and the Averages declined to 87 in December. They remained in a narrow range around the same level until March, 1915. Here an advance started, and prices reached 108 in November, 1915, finally working up to 112 in October, 1916. Note that this was the year of distribution in the rails, and that they only got three points higher in 1916 than the top of 1915, while industrials at the same time were having a big advance because war conditions were favoring industrials and working against the rails.

1917 was a year of big declines and great liquidation in the rails. Prices made the lowest for many years, declining to 71 in December, when the Government was forced to take over the railroads, which brought about a sharp rally in stocks. The averages advanced to 93 in November, 1918. Then came the end of the war, and they declined to 81 in January, 1919. Then followed the greatest industrial boom in the history of Wall Street, but rails failed to have any big advances, and only reached 92 in July and August, which was 1 point lower than the high prices of 1918; while industrial stocks advanced over 20 points higher than the 1918 prices, because industrials were now leaders and the rails were the laggards. In February, 1920, the rails declined to a new low level, making 68. After this, the rails and industrials began to work closer together. The rails rallied to 85 in November, 1920; then followed a long decline which carried them down to 66 in June, 1921, which was the lowest price at which the Averages had sold since 1897.

From this level, they advanced to 93 in August, 1922, which was the same top made in 1918. They remained at this same level during August, September, and October, 1922, holding in a narrow range while distribution was taking place. In November, they broke out of the distributing zone and declined to 82 on November 27. Since that time they have rallied to around 87 (January, 1923) where they are very dead and inactive, and meet selling on every rally. Every indication now seems to point to liquidation but the proper thing to do is to wait and see whether they become active and advance above the level of 86 or start activity on the down side and break under the level of 82 made in November. It is my opinion that before rails cross the 1922 highs again, they will sell at very much lower prices.

CHAPTER XXIV

BOTTOMS AND TOPS ON INDUSTRIAL STOCKS

Chart No. 12 shows the tops and bottoms on the Dow-Jones 20 Industrials from 1896 to December, 1922.

Note that the low in August, 1896 was 29. They rallied to 77 in April, 1899, where distribution started; declined to 68 in May; then rallied to 77 in September, 1899, making a double top; declined to 71 in October; rallied to 76 in November, failing to make the old top by one point. This was really a triple top, and failing to cross it showed big distribution and indicated a long decline to follow.

Prices declined to 58 in December; then rallied to 68, which was the bottom of the distributing zone. In 1903 during November and December, prices declined to 42 1/2, then rallied to 50 in January, 1904, and held in a 4-point range until June. They showed that accumulation was taking place, and that stocks were getting ready to advance, although at this time railroad stocks were the leaders. In July, 1904 the advance started, and continued, subject to minor interruptions, until January, 1906, where final top was made, prices reaching 103. This was a sharp top, and a decline followed, bringing prices down to 86 in July, 1906. They rallied to 96 in August and remained around the same level in a 4-point range, for about six months, until January, 1907. This showed big distribution in a narrow range and the long length of time indicated a big decline to follow.

1907 was a bear year in industrials as well as rails, and they declined to 53 in November, making a sharp bottom, as you will see from the chart. After this followed the long advance to the top in August, 1909. The industrials were now becoming more prominent, and were assuming the leadership over rails. Prices reached 100 in August, making a flat top, holding the same level for six months while dis-

135

CHART No. 12.—Dow—Jones' Averages, 20 Industrial Stocks. Monthly High and Low. 1897–1922

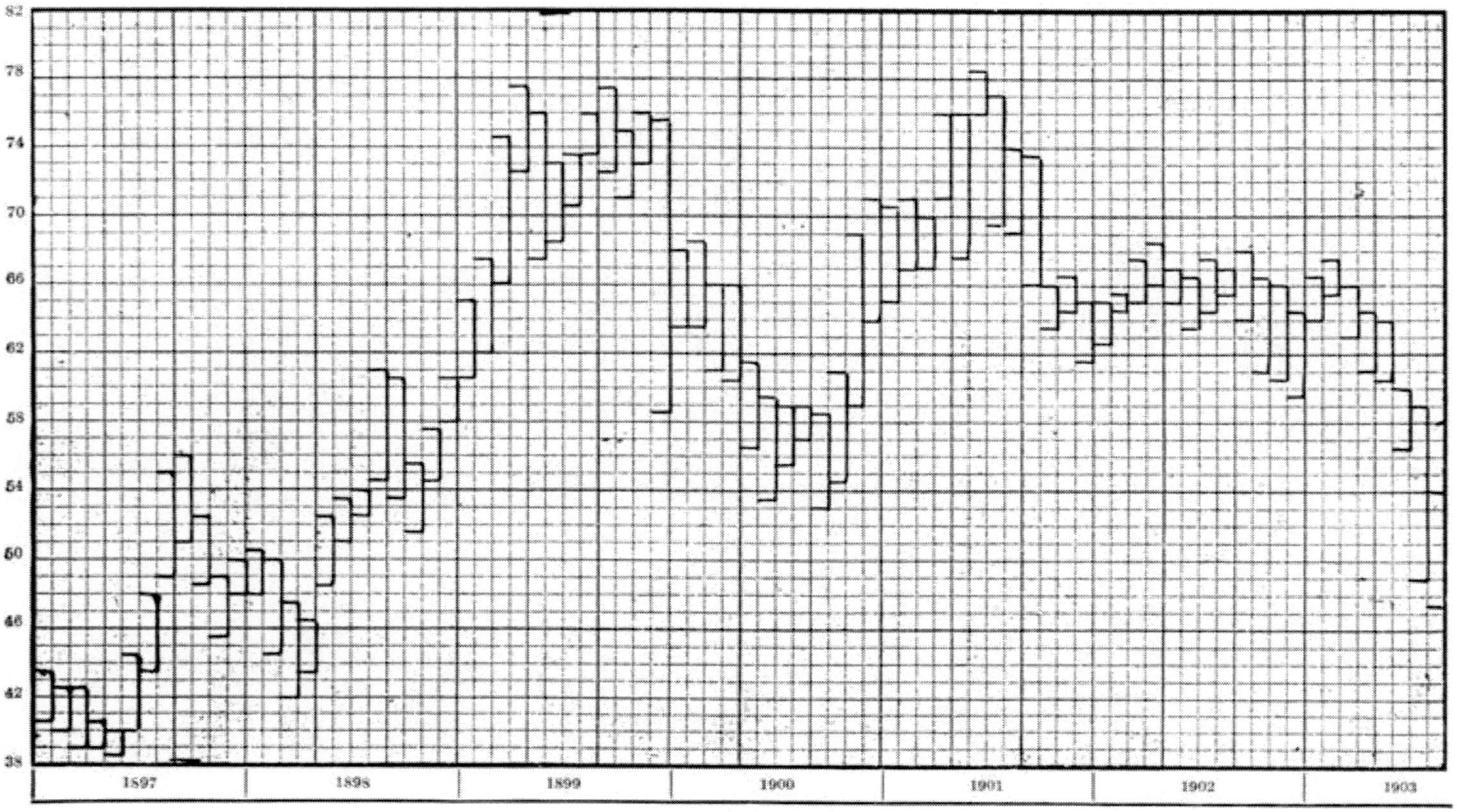

CHART NO. 12.—Dow-Jones' Averages, 20 Industrial Stocks. Monthly High and Low. 1897–1922—*Continued.*

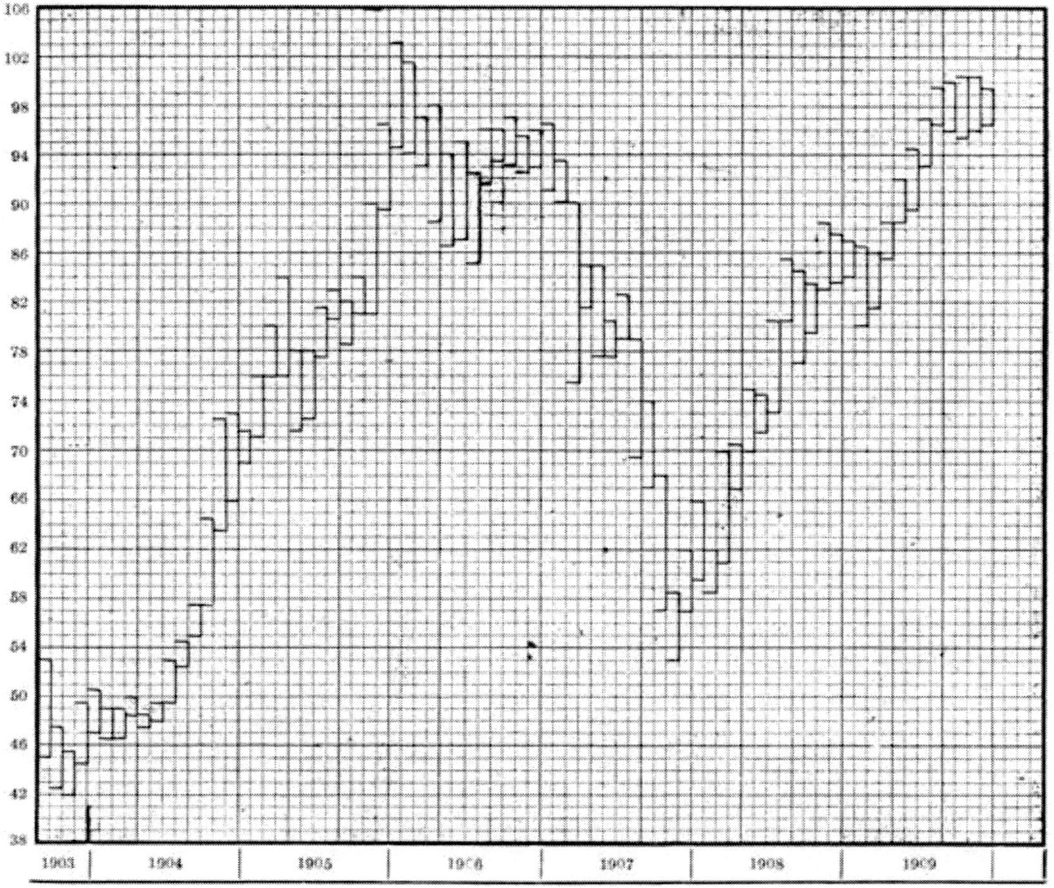

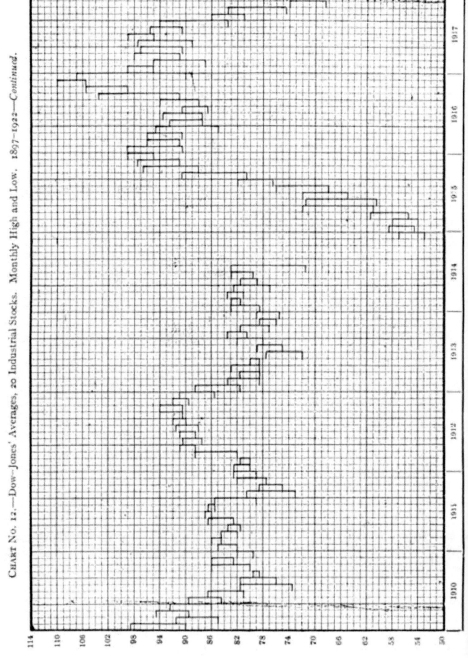

CHART No. 12.—Dow–Jones' Averages, 20 Industrial Stocks. Monthly High and Low. 1897–1922—Continued.

138

CHART No. 12.—Dow-Jones' Averages, 20 Industrial Stocks. Monthly High and Low.
1897–1922—*Continued.*

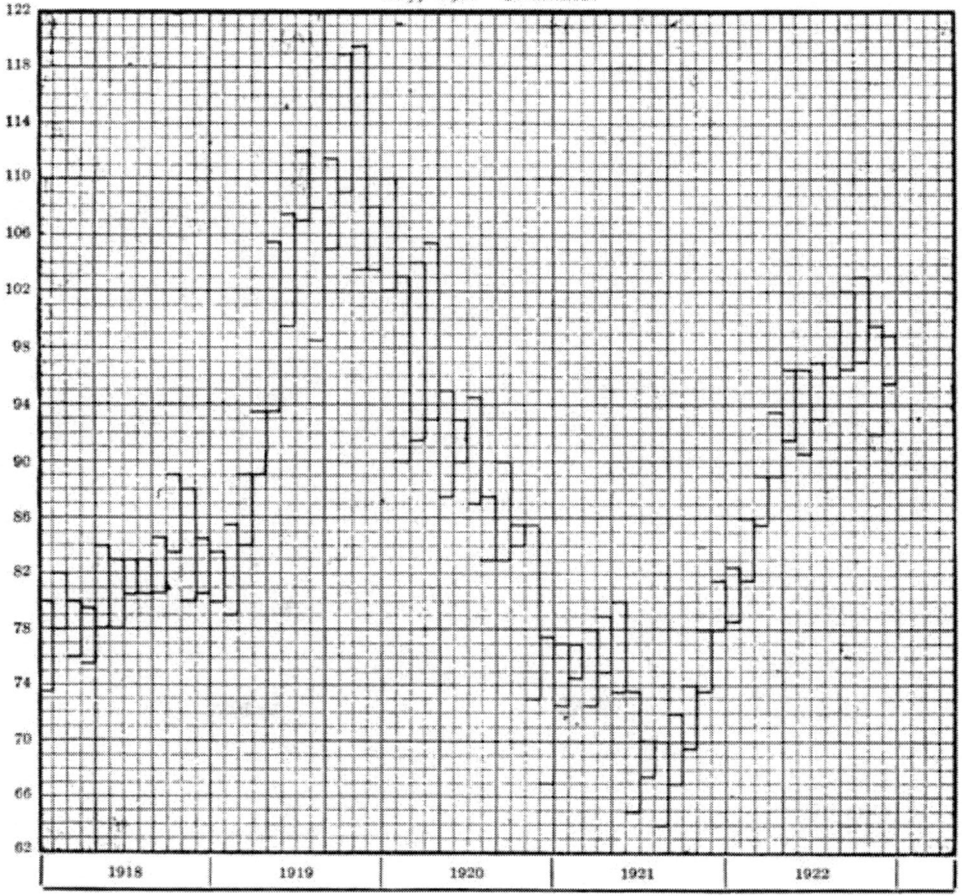

139

tribution was taking place. A decline started in January, 1910. Prices reached the low of 74 in July, 1910.

Then followed a slow rally, making top in July, 1911 and at the top the market remained for two months, very narrow and inactive, while distribution was taking place. You have often heard it said "Never sell a dead market," but you must consider whether prices are near the top or bottom when they become dead. If they get very narrow and dead near the top, it is a sign of decreased buying power, and only a question of time when something will occur to cause buyers to become sellers and force stocks down. The break started in August, and declined to 73 in September, 1911, making a double bottom.

Then followed a slow advance to October, 1912, the first top being made in June and the market holding about six months for distribution. Then followed a decline to June, 1913, when Averages reached 73, making a triple bottom, or practically the same level as 1910 and 1911.

In 1914 the top was made from February until July, in a very narrow market. Stocks would rally and become dead and inactive, which showed that the buying power was not there, and that liquidation was taking place. In the early part of July the decline started. Activity was on the down side, and prices broke under the distributing level. The Exchange closed July 30, and when it opened in December, prices declined to 53, making the same level as in 1907, or a double bottom, although it was seven years apart.

Prices fluctuated in a narrow range until the spring of 1915, when the industrial stocks led the advance, with "war babies" coming to the front every day. The Averages reached 99 in December, 1915, which was the first top in the great war boom. They declined to April, 1916, making 85. Here accumulation took place, and they rallied rapidly to November, 1916, when the Averages reached a new high for their history -- 110. From this top there was a sharp decline, and the real distribution took place under 100, or after stocks were down 10 points from high levels. I have explained something in regard to this in a previous chapter, about where sharp tops are made and distribution takes place after the first big decline.

In 1917 prices declined and reached the first low, 87, in February. They rallied from this level but were very inactive on the rallies. Stocks looked very cheap when compared to the high levels of 1916 and the public bought them. The decline continued during 1917 and bottom was reached in December, prices making 66. This was a sharp bottom. Then accumulation occurred after prices were up 10 points. The chart will show you that the accumulation took place between 76 and 84, so you see that the same rule applies -- *distribution takes place below the level of sharp tops and accumulation several points above the level of sharp bottoms.*

1918 was a year of narrow fluctuations. Prices had advanced to 88 in November, 1918, when peace was declared. Then followed a quick decline to 80, where you will see that prices held for four months in a 4-point range, making the same low level every month. This was the second stage of accumulation and showed that it was getting ready for a big advance, which started in February, 1919. You will find my Annual Forecast for 1919 in the back of this book. You can see how accurately I foretold the big advance in Oil Stocks and Industrials for that year. 1919 recorded one of the greatest advances in the history of the Stock Exchange, the industrial stocks rising nearly 40 points on Averages in nine months' time. Of course, many individual stocks had advanced from 50 to 150 points. The volume of sales was the greatest of any year on the Stock Exchange, the average daily sales running close to two million shares per day during August, September and October. In the early part of November, the advance culminated with a sharp top. There had been only two reactions during the year, one occurring in June and the other in August. Distribution took place on the way up, because the public was buying stocks regardless of price, name, previous condition or future possibilities. They were buying on hope, believing that the *Bull market* would never *end,* but it did, *suddenly and unexpectedly, as all highly manipulated market movements do.*

A panicky decline followed in November, 1919, and prices declined to around 103. They rallied and held in a narrow range, making 109 in January, 1920. A second period of distribution took place in January, which was fol-

lowed by a severe decline in February, carrying prices down
to 90. In April the Supreme Court handed down the deci-
sion declaring stock dividends non-taxable. This caused another wild wave of speculation, with many companies
declaring stock dividends and the public buying everything
on hope. The Averages reached 105 and from this level the
long decline started, which continued until December 21,
1920, winding up with a three million share day, and the
Averages at 67, the same level as they made in 1917. Read
my Annual Forecast in the back of the book, and see how
accurately I foretold the 1920 market and forecasted the
panicky decline to the exact date.

After this decline, a sharp rally followed to May, 1921,
when prices reached 81. The market became slow and dead
at the top, showing that the supply of stocks was greater
than the demand. Liquidation broke out again around the
10th of May, and prices continued to decline until liquidation
was completed in August and averages had reached 64. This
was the third zone below normal, or the zone of extreme
depression, and the place for accumulation and buying. It
was exactly opposite to the feverish zone of distribution of
October, 1919.

After the August, 1921, break, a slow rally started. See
my 1921 Stock Forecast in the back of this book. It called
the exact top for May and the bottom in August, 1921.

Reactions were very small and stocks continued upward
to October, 1922, when prices reached 103.42, where distribution started. The break which occurred in November,
1922, carried prices down to 92, which was 4 points under
the bottom of the distributing zone. My 1922 Stock Forecast, issued in December, 1921, called final high for October
to the exact date and predicted the decline for November,
1922.

You can see from the top that by January, 1923, distribution has been going on for about six months. They
rallied to just above 99 in January, 1923, and it is the writer's
opinion that the high prices made in October, 1922, will not
be exceeded by three points until Averages decline to 75 or
lower. Distribution will take place on every rally in the
Spring of 1923, and the Fall of 1923 will witness panicky
conditions in the stock market and drastic declines.

CHAPTER XXV

ACCUMULATION OF LOW-PRICED STOCKS

If you go back over past history, you will find that most of the stocks that have sold at very high levels, i.e., anywhere from $100 to $300 per share, at some time in the early stage of their career have sold at very low levels, and that the accumulation of many stocks which have become leaders has taken place below $25 per share. For example: See Chart No. 9 on Corn Products.

CORN PRODUCTS

In the great bull market of 1906, Corn Products sold at 28, which was the high price of that year. In the bear market of 1907 it declined to 8. In the bull market of 1909 it advanced to 26, failing by two points to reach the high price made in 1906. In 1911 it declined to 10 and in 1912 it advanced to 22, again failing to reach the high level of 1909. In 1914 it declined to 7, which was the lowest in its history. In 1915 it recovered rapidly and advanced to 21. In 1916 it advanced to 29, which was the highest price of its history up to that time, and one point higher than the level of 1906. 1917 was a bear year and many stocks sold lower than they had for many years, but Corn Products only reacted to 18 and before the end of 1917 had sold above 29, the highest of 1916. The stock being in new territory, and higher than it had sold for ten years, showed that accumulation had been completed and that a big advance was likely. Therefore the logical course to pursue was to follow the advance as long as the trend showed up.

It advanced to 37 late in 1917, thus making a new high in a bear year and showing that there was buying power enough to carry this stock up against the trend of the general

market. Now, when a stock has never sold higher than a
certain figure for a number of years, a lot of people think
that when it reaches that level or gets any higher, that it is
due for a reaction. This is a great mistake. 1918 was a
year of irregularities and reactionary price movements. It
could not be termed a bull year. Yet Corn Products advanced
to 50, and when other stocks suffered a big decline in January
and February, 1919 this stock only reacted to 46, or four
points from the high.

Then the 1919 bull campaign started and Corn Products
began to advance. It continued to make higher tops and
higher bottoms, showing that demand was greater than
supply, advancing to 99 in 1919, and in the spring of 1920
to 105. When it reached this level, if you look at a weekly
and monthly chart, you will see that distribution started. In
fact, it made a sharp top, reacted quickly to 88, then rallied
to 97, where it showed weakness. After that the trend was
down, and it declined to 61 in December, 1920; advanced to
76 in March, 1921; declined to 59 in June, 1921.

The fact that it only declined two points below the low
level made in 1920 and showed accumulation around this
level, it could naturally be considered in strong bull position
and should be bought with a stop under this low level. It
advanced to 68, reacted to 64, held in a narrow range between 64 and 68 while accumulation was taking place during
July and August, 1921. Then the advance started. It continued upward with very little reactions until it reached 105,
the high price of 1920. Of course, around this level it met
with heavy selling because a lot of people thought if it
reached the highest price of its history, it was high enough.

It advanced to 108 in March, 1922, which was three
points above the highest price made in 1920, and showed
that somebody was still buying the stock, although it was
meeting with heavy selling. It declined to 99 in May, 1922
and around this level became very inactive and the volume
of sales was very small, which showed that selling pressure
was decreasing. It started to advance slowly, and gradually
began to make higher resistance levels, until in August, 1922
it advanced above the high price of 108 made in March,
1922. After five or six months' time, and only reacting nine

points, then making a new high level, showed plainly that the trend was up and that the stock should be bought and followed up as long as it showed an upward trend.

It advanced to 134 during the week of October 21, 1922. After that it reacted to around 124; then rallied five or six times up to around 132-133, but failed to make the high price of October 21st. It remained in this trading range between 134 and 124, from October, 1922 until the date of this writing, January 12, 1923. This shows that it has reached the level where it is meeting with great resistance and heavy selling, and the proper thing to do is to be out of long stock, and short. If it breaks under the level of 124, it will show plainly that distribution has been completed, and you should then follow the downward trend until it reaches a level where it meets with resistance and shows accumulation.

CHAPTER XXVI

HOW TO WATCH INVESTMENTS

A lot of people handle their investments the same as they do their health. They never consult a doctor until they are seriously ill; then it may be too late, or the expense will be ten times greater than if they had consulted a doctor and protected themselves against future ailments. No matter if you hold gilt-edge bonds or preferred stocks as an investment, they should be looked over by an expert at least once a year to see if there are any symptoms of weakness developing in the list. Investments should be sold out on the first sign of a change in conditions, and you should not wait until everybody is selling and you are forced to sell on a liquidating market. Very few people are willing to pay even $25 a year to have their investments looked over, and receive real expert scientific advice, but after they have losses of thousands of dollars, and it is too late for expert advice to help them much, then they are willing to pay hundreds of dollars for helpful information. It is the old, old story of locking the stable door after the horse is stolen.

FRENCH BONDS

It is impossible for the best human judgment to pick a number of stocks or bonds that will all prove sound. It is also impossible to run any business without expense, and the expense in the investment business is occasionally taking a quick loss. When you find that one of your investments shows weakness, sell on the first indication -- do not hesitate. Many people bought French 7 1/2's and 8's above 100 because they pay 7 or 8 per cent. The very fact that they pay an abnormal yield on investments should have shown the man who thinks, that there was something wrong with the credit

146

of the French Government; otherwise they would not have
to pay such high interest if their security was gilt-edge.
When these bonds declined to 99 it was a danger signal and
they should have been sold out immediately, but many investors did not sell for the very reason that they yield a high
return. Now the 8's have declined to 93 and the 7 1/2's
around 89, and there is no prospect in sight for them going
back to par any time soon, so the man who bought because
he received a higher return for his money, now has a shrinkage in his capital of 7 to 10 per cent, which eats up a lot of
interest.

CHANGING TO SPECULATIVE ISSUES

It is always better to be safe than sorry. Many large
estates have been wiped out because the younger generation
refused to sell the investments that their fathers made and
switch into something better just as soon as the investments
began to show shrinkage. Many men leave fortunes to their
wives in gilt-edge investments which are paying 4 1/2 to 5 1/2
per cent. They have bought them for safety, for the protection of principal and not for large yield. A woman wants
a large income so that she can live on it. She will sell out
gilt-edge investments and buy speculative issues because the
return is large and often in a few years she finds herself not
alone without an income, but with her capital half wiped out.
The gambling instinct is so strong in human beings that they
never look for safety until it is too late. They listen to the
story of bond salesmen -- get-rich-quick schemers who play
on their hopes and get them to change from safe investments
into gambling speculative investments, and in 90 per cent of
the cases, the result is losses.

DISCRIMINATION AND INVESTIGATION

At the present time, when we are in a reconstruction
period after the greatest war the world has ever seen, dis-
crimination is more necessary than ever, and every investor
needs the service of an expert. Many people have the idea
that if they buy bonds which are sold by J. P. Morgan & Co.,

Kuhn Loeb & Company or the National City Bank, they are
buying something gilt-edge and guaranteed. These banks
are in the business of selling bonds for a commission. They
do not guarantee them, but they do make money on every
bond they sell. Yet, the buyer may never see a profit. The
very best houses must sometimes handle issues which are un-
sound, and you must not buy bonds without investigating
their merits just because they are sold by a house with a long
established reputation. The French Government issues were
all floated here by our highest class bankers, but that has not
prevented these bonds from shrinking in value, and the
bankers who sold you the bonds made no guarantee that they
would support the market and prevent a decline.

LIBERTY BONDS

The best securities are bound to shrink in value at times.
It is a question of Supply and Demand. The U. S. Government is the soundest government in the world today, and it
was at the end of the war in 1918. Then why did Liberty
Bonds decline to around 85? Because there were billions
of them in the hands of the public, and when the depression
of 1920 and 1921 set in, the people were loaded with bonds
and short of cash. Therefore, when they needed cash, the
only way to get it was to sell Liberty Bonds. The result
was that everybody were sellers and there were very few
buyers, and bonds declined. When they had been absorbed
at low levels by large investors, they gradually worked back
to 100 again.

ATCHISON

A lot of people have the idea that there is such a thing
as investments being so good that they cannot decline. They
forget the fact that Supply and Demand govern prices and
that there must be a buyer for every seller. If buyers are
scarce and sellers are numerous, stocks or bonds go down.
Suppose you were carrying Atchison Railway in 1915. It
advanced to 111, reacted to around 105, rallied to around
108, where you can see from a chart it held during 1916 and

part of 1917 without getting above this level. Here was an indication which showed plainly that the supply of the stock, after it made 111, was greater than the demand, and as the yield on the money invested was small compared to the high interest rate, the investor should have sold out Atchison and waited for a favorable opportunity to repurchase. On the break in the latter part of 1917 it declined to 75. During 1920 it held around 76, making the same level four or five times, which showed that it was receiving support and had reached a level where conditions were just opposite to what they were when the price was around 108. The demand was greater than the supply, and the stock stopped going down. After all the stock was absorbed at a low level, it started to advance, and again reached 108 in September, 1922, where it held for a short time without crossing the old level of 1916. This was the place to again sell out investments and wait. Atchison then declined to 98 in November, 1922. When it reaches a level where the demand is greater than the supply, it will again be time to buy. This may be several years off yet.

VALUE OF EXPERT ADVICE

You should keep a chart of all of your investments. It requires but little time to keep up a monthly high and low chart and it will show you when you should get out. If you are not sure of your own judgment, secure the services of a reliable expert whom you can depend upon. A lot of people feel that they cannot afford to pay out $100 to $200 each year for expert advice to protect their investments. If they would only look at it from a sensible standpoint, they would realize that they cannot afford to be without expert advice. Consider the price of my service -- $ 100.00 per year for my Annual Forecast on Stocks, together with a supplement issued once a month or more often. You have the privilege of asking my opinion at any time on any investment you hold and securing advice on how to switch your investments so that they will prove profitable and safe. The cost per year is one point on one hundred shares of stock. Many people carry thousands of shares and let their investments shrink thousands of dollars, when by paying $100.00 per year for my service, they would be able to save hundreds of times the amount they pay me.

Expert service works both ways. It not only protects you against loss, but helps you secure your profits at the right time. If you saw a plain indication that your health was breaking down, you would not wait until your case was hope-less, but would secure expert medical advice at once and be willing to pay a good price for it. Your investments, in one way, are more vital than your health, because if your invest-ments shrink to a level where they cause you to worry, you are sure to undermine your health. I have seen hundreds of cases in Wall Street where men lost their money, then lost their health. Therefore, expert scientific advice per-forms a double service -- provides protection for your health and your capital.

In Wall Street opportunities come more often than in
any other business, but you must have knowledge in order to
recognize them.

OPPORTUNITY

They do me wrong who say I come no more,
　　When once I knock and fail to find you in;
For every day I stand outside your door
　　And bid you wake and rise to fight and win.

Wail not for precious chances passed away,
　　Weep not for golden ages on the wane!
Each night I burn the records of the day;
　　At sunrise every soul is born again.

Laugh like a boy at splendors that have fled,
　　To vanished joys be blind and deaf and dumb;
My judgments seal the dead past with its dead,
　　But never bind a moment yet to come.

Though deep in mire wring not your hands and weep;
　　I lend my arm to all who say, "I can!"
No shame-faced outcast ever sank so deep
　　But yet might rise and be again a man!

Dost thou behold thy lost youth all aghast?
　　Dost reel from righteous retribution's blow?
Then turn from blotted archives of the past
　　And find the future's pages white as snow.

Art thou a mourner? Rise thee from thy spell,
　　Art thou a sinner? Sins may be forgiven,
Each morning gives thee wings to flee from hell,
　　Each night a star to guide thy feet to heaven.

-- WALTER MALONE.

BOOK IV

COMMODITIES

"There is a principle which is a bar against all information, which is proof against all argument, and which can not fail to keep a man in everlasting ignorance! That principle is condemnation before investigation." -- SPENCER.

CHAPTER XXVII

HOW TO TRADE IN COTTON

The cotton market offers good opportunities every year for making profits both as an investment and as a speculative proposition. Trading in future options is just as legitimate as buying and selling stocks. It is not necessary to buy the spot cotton outright, carry it in the warehouses, pay insurance and storage, for if spot cotton is going up or down, future options will fluctuate more than the cash article, and there is no expense in carrying futures outside of the margin requirements.

The course of cotton prices is based on supply and demand, and it is much easier to form a correct judgment on the cotton market than it is on the stock market, on account of there being so many stocks and different groups of stocks which cause a mixed trend, some stocks declining while others advance. With cotton it is different. If one option goes up, they all go up. You might be right on a certain group of stocks and yet pick the laggard to buy, and not make any money; but with cotton you could not miss it; if you were right on the trend you would make money. A man who trades in cotton with the proper capital and uses stop loss orders to protect his capital and also to protect his profits will be able to make more money than he will trading in stocks, especially when the cotton market is active.

The great trouble with the people in the Southern states, where cotton is grown, is that they are always bulls. They

never see but one side of the market and are always holding
on and hoping for it to go higher, no matter how high the
price advances. For this reason, 90 per cent of them lose
money simply because they are unwilling to see both sides
of the market. They ignore the bear side and refuse to
sell short in a bear market. I have known many traders to
buy cotton when it was high and lose anywhere from
$1,000 to $2,000 on 100 bales by simply sitting and
watching it decline day after day, and holding it for no other
reason than that they hoped it would go up. Remember my
rule -- *When you have nothing else to hold on for but hope,
get out quick.* Never trade without a reason. The time to
hold on is when the market is going in your favor and not
against you.

When cotton is at extreme high levels and starts downward, it goes down fast and continues down for a long time,
as past records will show. In the spring of 1920, cotton
was selling around 38 to 37 cents per pound, and in December same year, it sold below 15 cents per pound. Now,
what chance did a man have who was long of the market
and held on and hoped for a rally? The decline continued,
subject to rallies, until it got below the 11-cent level in June,
1921. Of course, the same rule applies to a man who sells
short against the trend and holds on and hopes. Cotton
was selling around 13 cents per pound in the middle of
August, 1921. The advance started and in thirty days it
advanced to around 21 1/2 cents per pound. Therefore, the
only thing to do in trading is to limit losses and go with the
trend. It is easy enough to make up a loss of 20 or 30 points,
but it is hard to make back losses of 200 to 400 points. Let
your rule be: *Cut short your losses and let your profits run.*
But remember, profits must be followed up with a stop loss
order, because it is just as foolish, after you have large
profits, to let them get away from you, as it is to lose part
of your capital by not protecting it.

REPORTS, NEWS, RUMORS AND VIEWS

Learn to discount reports which come from the farmers.
They are honest, but they have cotton to sell and are always

hoping for higher prices. They go to the extreme either way. If crops are bad, they exaggerate the damage. If crops are good, they are likely to become too hopeful and exaggerate the good condition. The man who produces the cotton to sell and the spinner who buys it are diametrically opposed to one another. Both are working for their own interests and you can not blame them, but you must discount their reports and opinions.

The tape tells you the consensus of opinion and reveals the predominance of the opposing forces and shows the trend according to supply and demand. Ignore the news, reports, opinions and views of everyone if it disagrees with what the chart and tape shows, for supply and demand must govern in the end, and if the selling power is greater than the buying, prices will decline, regardless of bad crop news or anything else. On the other hand, if the demand, or buying power, exceeds the selling, prices will advance regardless of good crop news. Of course, the general trend of the market does not continue for long contrary to natural conditions, but supply and demand govern the prices and the market discounts future events. Therefore, before you act too strongly on any good or bad news, be sure that your chart, which is but the reading of the tape and the correct interpretation of it, confirms the news and shows that it is yet to be discounted.

Do not try to trade too often. Jumping in and out of the market confuses you; the more trades you make the more chances you have for getting wrong, and increasing the percentage against you. You can always make profits if you wait for the opportunities. If you make two or three consecutive trades and they go against you, and you have to take losses, better quit for awhile and look on. Wait until your judgment gets clear, and the market shows a definite trend. You can always form a better judgment when you are out of the market than when you are in it, because you are not influenced by your hopes and fears.

It makes no difference whether you trade on the New Orleans Cotton Exchange, N. Y. Cotton Exchange or in Liverpool, the trend of the market is always the same, once it shows conclusively that a move has started. Liverpool may go contrary to New York for one day, but it seldom

ever goes two. The same with New York or New Orleans.
They always run on a very close parallel.

AMOUNT OF CAPITAL REQUIRED

One of the most important things that traders overlook
is the amount of capital required to make a success trading
in cotton. A lot of people think that when cotton is around
the normal level, from 9 cents to 12 cents per pound, that
$200 or $300 is enough capital to use in trading in 100
bales. This is financial suicide, because if a man loses
20 or 30 points on the first trade, his capital is crippled so
that he cannot make a second trade. A man should go into
the cotton market the same as he goes into any other business, -- to make a success and not a gambling proposition. If
you make speculation or investment a business, you probably
will be able to accumulate a fortune over a number of years,
but if you go into it to gamble and expect to make it all on
one deal, you will lose all your money and have nothing left
but hope.

When cotton is at an abnormal high level, as it has been
since 1915, selling between 15 cents and 40 cents per pound,
it requires a larger amount of capital because stop loss orders
will be caught more frequently and at the same time profits
will be much greater. I consider $2,000 the amount of
capital that should be used for trading in 100 bale lots.
Nothing less is safe. This money is not to be used to put
up on 100 bales and hold it if it starts going against you.
It is for the purpose of paying several small losses and still
have capital enough left to continue to trade until you hit it
right and begin to make big profits.

HOW STOP LOSS ORDERS SHOULD BE USED

In normal markets, when fluctuations are narrow, you
should use a stop loss order not more than 20 points away.
In very wild active markets, where fluctuations are wide, you
should use a stop loss order about 40 points away, but a risk
of $200 should be the maximum on any one deal. If
your capital is $2,000 and you make five trades and lose
half of your capital and then make one trade which shows

a profit of 200 points, you would be even. Most people trade the other way -- They take 20 to 40 points' profit and 200 to 300 points' losses. There is no chance of beating the cotton market that way. Of course, before you make a trade, you should try to determine the trend and be as near right as possible, but if you see that you are wrong, there is one sure way to play safe and that is get out at the market or place a stop loss order for your protection which will automatically put you out.

Once you make up your mind and place a stop loss order, do not cancel it, or change it to where you have a greater loss if it is caught. In 99 cases out of 100, you will be wrong when you place yourself in a position to take a greater loss than you first decided on. It may be well enough some times to cancel orders for taking profits if the market is going your way, but never cancel an order to stop a loss. The sooner a loss is stopped the better both for your capital and for your judgment. As long as you stay in the market and a trade goes against you, your judgment gets worse all the time; in fact, you have no judgment. It is simply a big hope that the market will turn and go your way.

HOW TO PYRAMID

In rapid markets successful pyramiding can be carried on. Of course, the condition of the market has to determine how close pyramids can be made safely. As a rule, after you buy 100 bales, you should not buy the second lot until the market has moved 60 points in your favor. Then place a stop loss order on your 200 bales so that if the stop is caught you will not lose as much money as your original risk on the first 100 bales.

We will assume that on the first 100 bales, you place a stop loss order 40 points away, which would be a loss of $200. Now, when you buy or sell the second 100 bales, place a stop loss order 40 points away on 200 bales. If the stop is caught, you will lose 40 points on the last 100 bales, but will make 20 on the first 100 bales, which places you in a better position than if the first trade had gone against you. If the market continues to move in your favor and your stop

loss order is not caught, you can continue to buy or sell on
the way up or down, but don't forget that the more the
market moves in your favor, the nearer the end of the move
is over, and buying must not be increased near the top after
a long move, nor selling increased near the bottom after a
long decline.

STRADDLES OR HEDGING ON COTTON

Many cotton traders get the idea that they can sell one
option and buy another, thereby making a straddle which
will work closer together and show them a profit. In nine
cases out of ten, it works exactly opposite, and instead of a
profit the result is a big loss. If you cannot form a judgment
of the trend of the market, then do not try to play both
sides at the same time. Something always happens to upset
all calculations when traders figure out a dead sure cinch on
a straddle. As a trader once said to me, "My broker recom-
mended something safe and sure -- a good straddle -- and I
got on for a joy ride and the straddle tore both my legs off."
This is the way most straddles work out.

Another great mistake that traders make is that when
they buy one option and it starts to go against them, they
refuse to see that they are wrong and accept a loss, but sell
another option to hedge. Then they are both long and short
of the market, and they have to make two guesses as to
where they will get out right. It can not be done. They
invariably close the trade that shows a profit and hold the
one that shows a loss. In this way, they undo the wrong
side of the hedge. A man can not have a clear judgment
trying to play two sides of the market at the same time. It
is bad enough playing one side. Therefore, keep out of
hedges and straddles; try to determine the trend and follow it.

CHAPTER XXVIII

PROPER WAY TO READ THE COTTON TAPE

The cotton market, as I stated before, is governed by Supply and Demand. The only difference in reading the tape on cotton and reading it on stocks is that the cotton tape does not show the number of bales traded in on each sale. This makes it a little difficult at times to determine the trend, but while we do not know the amount of trading that is going on, the fluctuations on the tape show very plainly whether the volume is extra heavy or very small. The market does not stand still on large buying or selling; it moves one way or the other. Therefore the activity tells us whether or not there is big business going on. When fluctuations are very narrow and the market is dull and inactive, it shows that the buying and selling is reduced to a small scale, and no big move is indicated. Therefore, the only thing to do is to watch and wait until you see activity start, and then go with it.

The best way to read the cotton tape is the same as stocks -- stay away from it; keep up a chart and read the tape quietly, away from the influence of the broker's office and the gossip which is always prevalent there, that will mix your judgment and invariably cause you to see things in the wrong light.

The cotton tape fools you just as often as the stock tape, because local weather condition, good or bad, will cause quick declines or advances which in no way change the major trend. Yet, while looking at the tape, it will appear extremely strong or weak and at the time you are convinced and act upon it. Afterwards you find that you have bought at the top or sold at the bottom, and then when the main trend is resumed, you are wrong, and of course, the tape whispers hope and you hold on. If you are away from it, you will make your trades according to your rule, place your stop loss orders, and will

not be influenced by hope or fear. The same rule applies
in narrow markets as in markets of wide fluctuations. Distribution has to take place before any important decline and
time has to be allowed for accumulation before any big advance takes place.

DISTRIBUTION OR TOP ZONE

Chart No. 13 on cotton shows the October option from
November, 1919 to January, 1923, that is, all important
tops and bottoms, accumulation and distribution. Notice
that from December 6, 1919 to December 13, it declined
from 2970 to 2700. Then followed an advance up to 3140
on January 17, 1920; then a decline to 2760 on February 7.
The following week the market started to rally, after making
a higher bottom than the one in December. After that note
the progressive bottoms and tops. The advance continued,
every week making higher, until the week of April 17 it
advanced to 3715. The following week, ending April 24,
it advanced to 3725, which was the final high. It declined
quickly to 3430, but as distribution had not been completed,
it required time. The market fluctuated up and down over
a wide range, running up near the 37-cent level several
times. On May 22, it advanced to 3690; then declined to
3410, and on June 5 made the last rally to 3670. After
that it declined to 3170 on July 3; then rallied to 3530 on
July 24, but the decline on July 3, as you will see, had broken
under the distributing level, which indicated that the big
trend had turned down and that cotton was a short sale on
all rallies.

LIQUIDATION

A rapid decline followed, which carried prices down to
2550 on September 4, 1920, followed by a rally to 2960
on September 8. Note the following week was a narrow
range. Then the decline started again, and drastic liquidation continued, carrying prices down to 1440 during the week
ending November 27. After this the market rallied to 1650;
declined to 1360 on January 1, 1921, rallied to 1640 Janu-

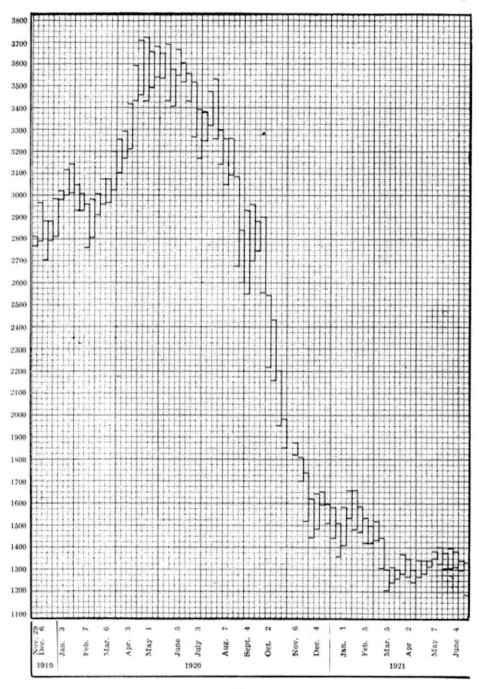

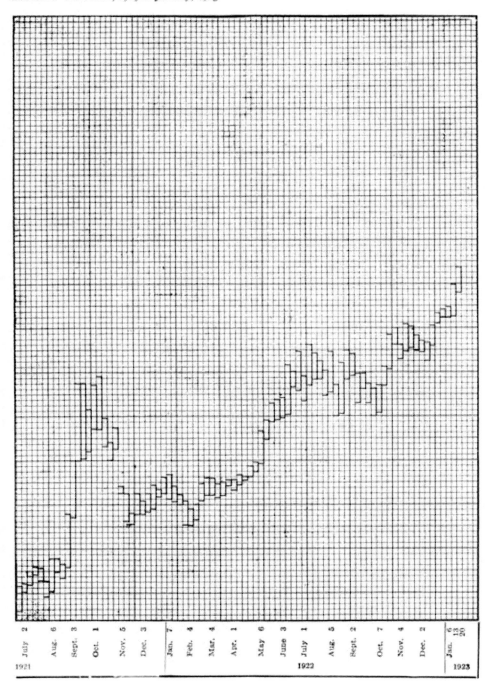

ary 22, which was slightly above the top on December 18, 1920, where it again met selling. Notice that fluctuations were narrowing down, but bottoms were getting lower and tops also decreasing. The decline continued to March 5, and prices reached 1200. A slow rally followed, prices getting back, as you will see, to the 14-cent level during May and early June. Then followed another decline down to 1120, making final low on June 25.

ACCUMULATION

This was a sharp bottom and a quick rally followed, which carried prices to 1320 on July 16, 1921; then a reaction to 1190 on July 30; followed by a rally which carried prices up to 1350 on August 6, for the first time since prices broke under 30 cents per pound making a higher top after an important new low level. Here the market rested for a couple of weeks and then advanced above the August high. This was the cue that the trend had changed and that it was time to buy, because after several months of narrow fluctuations at a low level, prices became very active on the advance. Now when the 14-cent level was crossed, which was above all of the tops made in May and June, it was another sure indication that a big move was on, and this would be the place to pyramid. Prices advanced rapidly in September, and crossed the high levels around 1650 which were made in December, 1920, and January, 1921. The advance was rapid, and by September 10 had reached 2150. Then followed a sharp reaction to around 1810. This is where your stop loss order would have put you out when the reaction started.

You can not expect a big move upward or downward to start until after accumulation or distribution has taken place. The market halted for a few days above the 18-cent level, then rallied right back to 2150. This would have been the place to go short with a stop loss order 30 to 40 points above the old top. After this, prices again declined to around 1930 where they became dull and narrow. The advance started again and on October 8, 1921, rallied, making a slightly higher top at 2175. A decline started and

continued downward till prices reached 1520 the week ending
November 19. Then a slow rally for several weeks, carrying prices up to 1730 on January 7, 1922; followed by a
decline to 1510, making a double bottom against the low of
November 19, 1921. This would be your buying point with
a stop loss order 30 to 40 points under the previous bottom.

SECOND STAGE OF BULL MARKET

After this, a slow advance started. On February 25,
1922, prices were up to 1720, just under the high price made
in January. A reaction followed carrying prices to around
1640, where the market became very dull and narrow. In
this position you should wait and see whether prices broke
under the level made on the first reaction during the week
of March 4, or whether they advanced above the high price
made on January 7. During the week ending April 22, prices
crossed the high level made in January and March. This
showed that the trend had turned up, and as big accumulation
had taken place over a long period of time, you could expect
a big advance. The trend continued upward until June 24,
when prices reached 2290. Then followed a sharp decline
down to 2070; then a quick advance up to 2325. Here the
market became narrow and dull around the top levels and
you should have sold out and gone short.

RESISTANCE LEVEL

A decline followed to 2090 during the week of July 29,
1922; then an advance to 2290 the week of August 5, followed by a sharp decline down to 2000; then a rally to 2290
on August 26, prices again failing to get above the high
levels made in the early part of July and August. This indicated distribution around the 23-cent level, and you should
sell out and go short with stop 30 to 40 points above old
tops. A decline followed, carrying prices down to 2000
again during the week ending September 30. 2000 was the
level reached on August 12, and you should cover shorts and
wait, or you could buy with a stop loss order 30 to 40 points
under this level, which was not broken.

THIRD STAGE OF BULL MARKET

An advance started, the market moving up rapidly, carrying prices above the 23-cent level, and over all of the tops made in July and August. This was an indication that prices were going higher. They reached 2400 the week of October 28, 1922. Then they declined to 2260; rallied to a new high, 2415, but became narrow and dull and your stop loss order would have been caught on a reaction. The next point to watch was the last low level made on November 4. When prices reached this level the week of December 9, you should have bought with stop loss order 30 to 40 points lower and your stop would not have been caught. After this, the advance was resumed, the market continuing to make higher prices until the October option reached 2677 on January 24, 1923, the date of this writing. After distribution is completed at these high levels, a long decline will start which will carry prices back to the 15-cent level or lower.

This chart is all you need to learn about reading the tape on fluctuations in cotton, because the same principles are followed whether the market is a narrow normal market or an abnormal market selling at extremely high prices. I have simply used this chart to illustrate the principle of trading. You can apply it to any other option or any period in the past or future, and will find the market working out the same.

It always pays to trade in the active options, and not trade when they get too close to maturity. There is no use taking chances on wild fluctuations and bad executions when you get near delivery dates. Trade in the next option where you can get good executions.

CHAPTER XXIX

HOW TO DETERMINE A CHANGE IN TREND

When the market is fluctuating in a very narrow range, you should keep up a chart of every 10-point move made during the day. In this way you will be able to see whether accumulation or distribution is taking place, and discern where resistance levels are formed. When it breaks out into new territory you can then follow the trend. In very active markets, when prices are high and the range wide, fluctuations of 10 points mean very little, and you should keep a chart of every move of 30 to 40 points made during the day. In this way you will be able to locate the resistance levels and tell when it breaks out of the zone of accumulation or distribution.

You should always keep a monthly, weekly, and daily high and low chart on the active options you are trading in. It will only require fifteen to twenty minutes each day to do this and you will be well repaid for your trouble. The value of charts is to determine where support is given and where it is withdrawn; also where resistance is met on an advance and where it is overcome, thus enabling you to buy and sell and place a stop loss order as close as possible for your protection.

After violent fluctuations up or down, the market nearly always comes to a standstill before the next move starts. Buying and selling becomes about equal and the market narrows down, then activity starts one way or the other and you should go with it. Of course, there are bound to be false moves at times. After accumulation is shown some news may develop which will cause a sharp drive down, followed by a quick rebound. Then if prices go above the levels previously established, you can consider that the move has reversed and that prices will continue upward.

Often when the first top is made, a lot of profit taking will be encountered and a short interest will be built up. Something will occur of a favorable nature to scare the shorts and they will cover, forcing prices to a slightly higher level, which weakens the technical position. Then a quick decline will start, and if previous low levels are broken and the market is very active on the decline, it will be an indication that the trend has again turned down.

Do not try to trade every day. Watch and wait for opportunities and once you see you are in right and with the trend of the market, follow it up or down until you see a sign that the trend has reversed. Do not close your trade just because you have a profit, but always be convinced by the position of the chart and the general condition, that the trend has changed. Never buy after a lot of very bullish news comes out, nor sell after an extremely bearish report. Both good and bad news is nearly always discounted. Of course, consider whether the trend is up or down when good or bad news is made known.

Never try to start to pyramid after a long advance or decline. The chances are against you. Begin pyramiding when the trend first turns up or down after long moves. When prices reach top or bottom, as a rule, a series of rapid fluctuations take place; then the market gradually narrows down and lays the foundation for another important move.

If prices are high in the spring of the year, after a very short crop, be very careful about buying, as a decline may start which will discount a new crop six months later. The same applies to selling short in the spring following a very large crop. If prices are low, they have already discounted the old crop, but have yet to discount the future, which may be more favorable or unfavorable. After everybody knows about a large crop, or an extremely short one, it is too late to trade on it to advantage, except on rare occasions, and your chart will always show you when these changes are taking place at high or low levels.

Do not sell cotton short just because it may be at a very high price. Remember it can always go higher if conditions are right. Neither buy it just because it is at a low level, as it can always go lower. Never buck the trend, and do not try to guess the top or bottom. Wait until the chart shows you that the trend has turned. You can always make plenty of money buying or selling after the trend is well defined. The man who is in too big a hurry will lose money and miss opportunities just as often as the man who is too slow to act.

CHAPTER XXX

THE BOLL WEEVIL

This little pest began his ravages on cotton in Texas
about twenty years ago. He has grown gradually worse,
working further north every year until he finally crossed the
Mississippi, doing great damage in the Southern cotton-grow-
ing states. Man has used all of his resources at hand to
destroy this little monster and at the present writing everyone seems to think that the boll weevil is unconquerable. It
reminds me of 1893, when cotton was selling at 4 cents per
pound and people were disgusted and leaving their farms.
Uncle Henry said "Things are so bad that something has
to be done. You can't beat that old head of a man for
figuring out things." Of course, after fields were abandoned
and people went to the saw-mills to work, crops decreased
and prices went up. When conditions go to the extreme one
way or the other, something always happens and men get
busy, start thinking, and figure out a way to bring about a
change.

In 1917, when the English and French had their backs
to the wall, and Germany was driving them rapidly back,
the time had come when something must be done, and it was
Uncle Sam's boys that turned the tide and saved the day.
The American people, while extravagant, are resourceful in
many ways, and every age produces its genius. Whenever
we reach extremes and there is a great demand for brains,
they are always forthcoming. Millions of dollars have been
raised recently to solve the problem and exterminate the boll
weevil and there is no doubt but that the man of the hour,
some American genius, will appear with a new invention or
destructive poison, which will spell doom to the little boll
weevil. Then the bulls who were talking and hoping for
40 cents and 50 cents per pound on cotton, like the boll

weevil, will pass away and the bears will again reign supreme with cotton back in the "teens."

Cotton has held at high levels since 1915, when the advance started from 7 cents per pound. I remember well in the Fall of 1914 when the South was in deplorable condition, and they were urging everyone "to buy a bale." Cotton could only be sold for about $30 per bale, but to save the South, people were urged to buy it at $50 per bale. I recall, one night I was in the McAlpin Hotel, and in the lobby there was a bale of cotton with a big sign on it: "Buy a bale and help save the South." This was the extreme of over-production -- big supply and small demand; of course, helped by the outbreak of the war, which temporarily stopped European buying.

With cotton around 29 cents a pound, and having been higher for many years, people are convinced that the boll weevil is the "Kaiser" of the hour, and that cotton can never be grown again in sufficient quantities to supply the demand. But a change will come, and a supply in excess of the demand will be produced. Why? Because there is big money in growing cotton at 25 cents per pound. People will always go into a business where money can be made, and over-production is sure to come. It is the other extreme which must follow the present conditions of small supply and large demand. I have no hesitancy in predicting that a large crop will be grown in 1923 and that before the spring of 1924 cotton will sell at the 15-cent level and in a few years will again be below 10 cents per pound.

When extremes occur and everybody is radically bearish and can see no hope for prices ever advancing, or when prices are abnormally high and everybody believes that conditions are such that there is no hope for prices ever going down, that is the time to go against human judgment and follow the tape and charts, for they will point to the correct course of prices according to the natural law of supply and demand.

CHAPTER XXXI

WHEAT AND CORN TRADING

The Wheat and Corn markets, like Cotton, are easier
to follow than stocks, as I have explained before, because
they are less confusing. Once you determine the trend, all
options move with it. If you buy or sell and are correct on
the trend, you will make profits; while in trading in stocks,
you might be correct on the trend of rails, for instance, but
if you picked the laggard stocks to buy or sell, you would
make very little money or might even have a loss, although
you were right on the trend. This can never happen when
trading in grain. Therefore, it is well to make a careful
study of the commodity market, as it offers several opportunities every year for making substantial profits when the
seasonal moves take place.

ABNORMAL MARKETS

Remember that abnormal markets, with wide fluctuations, only occur years apart. Therefore you must not expect
unreasonable profits in normal times. During the past seven
years, or since the war broke out, we have had abnormal
markets, and Wheat and Corn have made a wide range of
fluctuations, much greater than can ever be expected in
normal times. Many traders miss opportunities for fair
profits at the present time because they are looking and hoping for war profits. There is no reason or sound basis for it.
They are simply gambling on hope.

The price of Wheat, Corn and Oats is to a great extent
determined by the purchasing power of the dollar. The
farmer could make more money in 1895 and 1896 growing
Wheat and selling it at 60 cents per bushel, than he can
selling it today at $1.00 per bushel, because the purchasing

power of the dollar has decreased. Labor and land values have increased. When these conditions change and farm labor is again back to normal, Wheat and Corn, as a natural consequence, will seek lower levels. All of these factors which govern natural conditions must be considered in judging the trend of a market.

CAPITAL REQUIRED

The amount of capital depends upon whether Wheat is in a narrow range in a normal year or making wide fluctuations in an abnormal year. I consider that at least $2,000 should be used under any condition for trading in 5,000-bushel lots. Then, if you limit your losses to 2 cents to 3 cents per bushel, you can make enough trades on your capital to continue until your profits exceed your losses.

Suppose you use a stop loss order about 4 points away, which would mean a loss of $200 on each 5,000-bushel lot. This would enable you to make ten trades on your capital. If you made five trades and they all showed losses, you would still have plenty of margin to make another trade, and if you were successful in working with the trend, two trades that are right should wipe out five losses.

In a normal market you should use about $1,000 for each 5,000 bushels of Corn that you trade in. Losses should be limited to about 2 cents per bushel and stop loss orders should never be more than 3 cents per bushel away. It is not safe to risk more than 3 cents on any one trade. If you are wrong, you should get out and wait.

STOP LOSS ORDER FOR PROTECTION

In trading in Wheat or Corn, stop loss orders should always be used on every trade. The man who trades without a stop loss order will sooner or later lose all his money. As a rule, it never pays to risk more than 2 cents to 3 cents per bushel on any one trade, and even in abnormal wild markets not more than 5 cents per bushel. If you can not guess the top or bottom within 5 cents per bushel, you are wrong and should get out and wait for a change in trend.

Never buck the trend, because your stop loss orders will
be caught more often. In a bull market, always buy on a
reaction; in a bear market, sell on rallies. Do not try to
guess when the market has reached top or bottom, but wait
until the tape shows it. Give the market time, and supply
and demand will tell you when the trend has definitely
changed.

PYRAMIDING

In active markets, you can pyramid. The distance between your trades in pyramiding depends, of course, upon
the market. In a narrow market, you should not buy or sell
a second lot until after the first trade has moved 4 cents to
5 cents in your favor. In markets like we had during the
war, you can pyramid about every 7 cents to 10 cents per
bushel up or down. In normal markets, when Wheat moves
10 cents to 12 cents per bushel, you can always expect a
reverse move of from 3 cents to 5 cents per bushel. Therefore, you have to be careful about buying or selling on the
bottom or top of a 10-cent move.

Once the market gets away from the accumulation period
and the trend is well defined up or down, reactions are very
small. While accumulation or distribution is taking place,
you should trade for small scalping profits, and never attempt
to start to pyramid. Wait until the accumulation or the
distribution zones are cleared before buying or selling a
second lot.

CHAPTER XXXII

JUDGING ACCUMULATION AND DISTRIBU-
TION ZONES

The same rules that apply to stocks and cotton apply to grain. Before any move of great importance or of long duration takes place, time is required for accumulation or distribution. In an active option, you should keep up a daily high and low chart, a weekly, and a monthly chart. The daily chart will enable you to tell when the minor moves start, which only last for a few days; while the weekly and monthly charts will enable you to determine when there is a change in the major trend, and thus you can buy or sell in time to catch the big moves.

MONTHLY RANGE OF WHEAT PRICES

Supply and demand govern the course of commodity prices, but the tape, or a chart, which reveals the concentrated buying or selling power, will show which way the main trend is moving.

In 1894 and 1895 Wheat sold at 50 cents per bushel, which was the lowest since the Civil War. Prices did not advance rapidly but held at low levels for several years. Note Chart No. 14 from 1895 to 1898. The bottom on May Wheat was made at 56 cents in December, 1895; then rallied to 68 cents in February, March and April, 1896; declined to 56 cents in May, 1896, the same level made in December, 1895. After that, prices crossed the 68-cent level, which was above the distribution zone, and advanced to 85 cents, where you will notice they made the same level of tops for four months. Then followed a decline to 64 cents in April, 1897. After this, the advance started, which carried prices above 85 cents, the highest they had been for several years. Prices reached $1.00 per bushel in August,

CHART NO. 14.—May Wheat, Monthly High and Low. 1895–1904

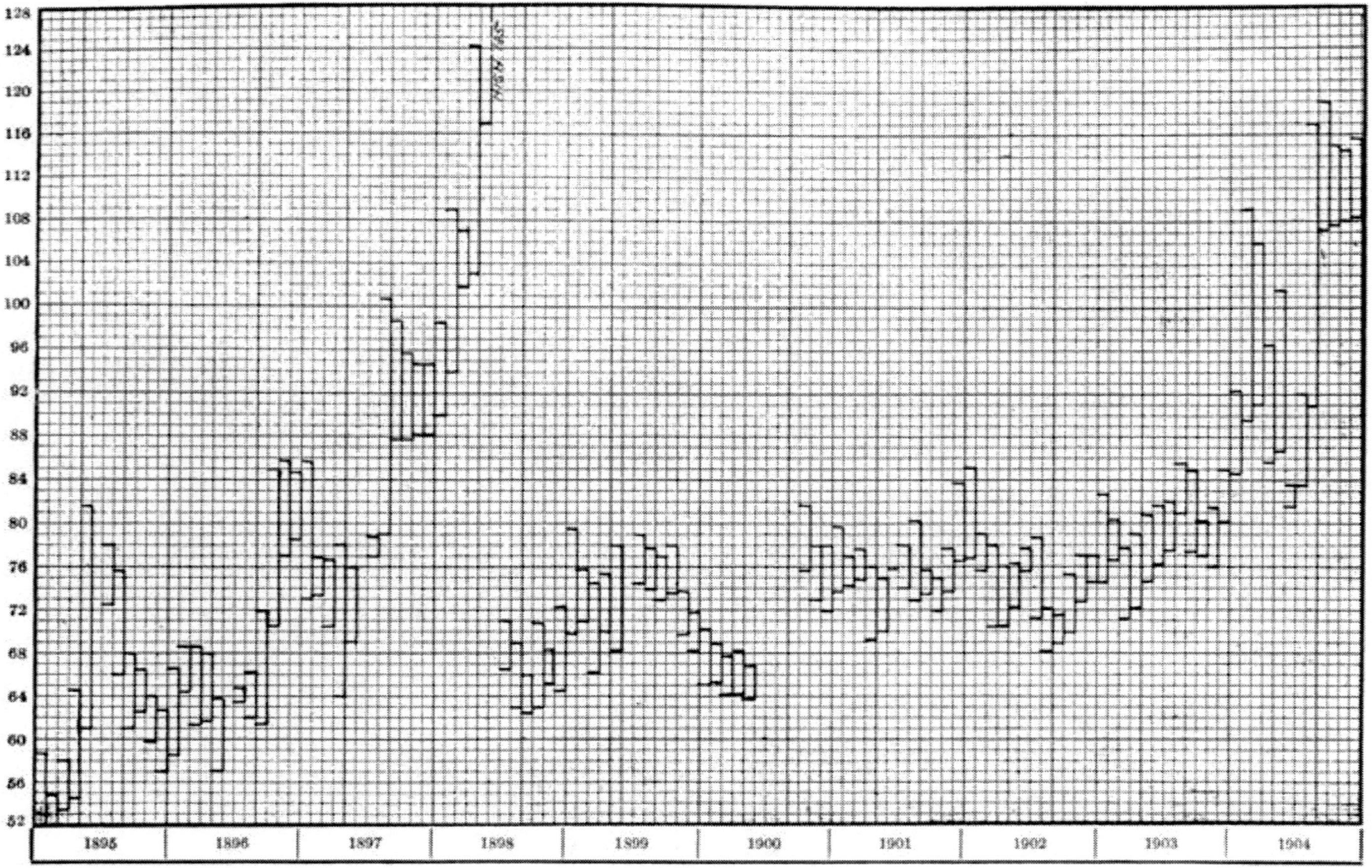

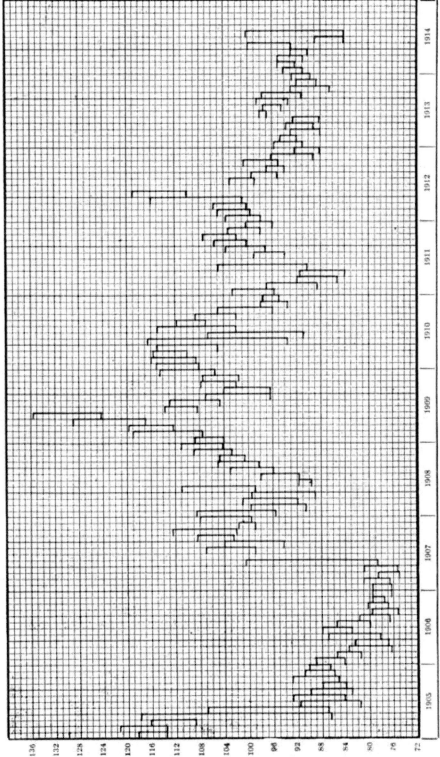

175

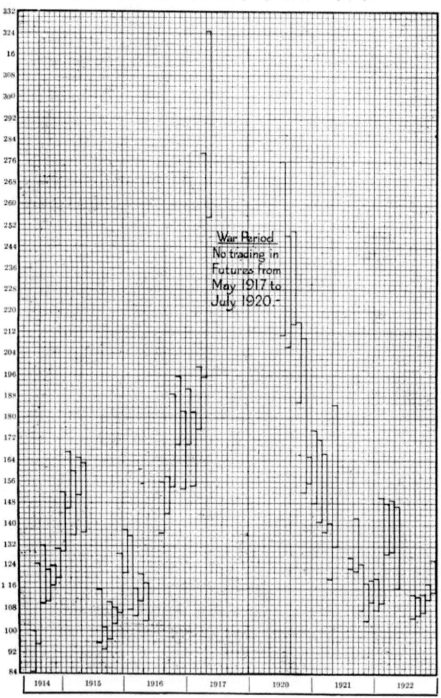

War Period
No trading in
Futures from
May 1917 to
July 1920.-

1897; then reacted to 88 cents, fluctuating in a narrow range between 88 cents and 95 cents for four months. In December, 1897, prices advanced to 98 cents which was above the high level for the past four months.

Remember we have stated that before any big advance or decline takes place, there must be a long period of time for accumulation or distribution before the move starts. From August, 1897, until February, 1898, accumulation had taken place at a level above the high prices for several years past. In other words, prices were maintained at a level which was really a new high level of values, for a period of seven months, and once the trend turned and advanced above $1.00, it continued up to 1.09, showing a big move was on. During the month of March, 1898, trading was in a narrow range between 1.07 and 1.02 for the May Option, but every indication showed that the trend was up. Then the big advance started which carried May Wheat to 1.85 in May, 1898. This was the Leiter Corner. Mr. Leiter had accumulated a large line of Wheat but was unable to sustain prices at a high level, with the result that the Corner collapsed and Wheat immediately broke back below $1.00 per bushel.

In September, 1898, notice that May Wheat again declined to around 62 cents per bushel. It held for three months around this level and in January, 1899, advanced to 79 cents. After that the market was a narrow, normal affair and prices again advanced to around 79 cents in July and September, 1899; then declined to 64 cents in March, April and May, 1900, where you can see that the fluctuations narrowed down to 3 or 4 cents per month.

SWING CHART

After that followed a long period of narrow fluctuations, but you will note from Chart No. 15, which shows only the big swings -- major tops and bottoms -- that from the early part of 1895 prices continued to work higher every year; that is, making a slightly higher bottom every time, until the war broke out in 1914, which again carried prices to abnormal high levels, reaching 3.25 in May, 1917.

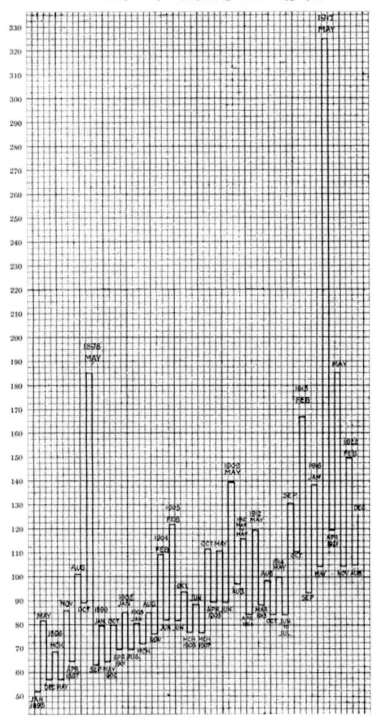

178

Notice the top in the fall of 1904 and the early part of 1905, when Wheat reached 1.20, which was the highest price since the Leiter Corner. Note that distribution took place between 1.08 and 1.20, and that when prices broke below this level, they rapidly declined, reaching 82 cents in June, 1905. This is what always follows a long period of accumulation or distribution. Once prices break out of the accumulation or distribution zone, a rapid move follows.

Note the bottom made between March, 1906, and April, 1907 -- a period of twelve months in a very narrow range. In September, 1906, prices declined to 75 cents and never rallied above 81 cents until May, 1907, a period of nine months of accumulation in a very narrow range. In May, 1907, when prices advanced to 82 cents they were out of the accumulation zone and immediately moved up rapidly to $1.00 in May, and on the Green Bug scare in October, 1907, Wheat sold at 1.12.

Note on Chart No. 15 that the low price on Wheat in April, 1911, was 84 cents and that it advanced to 1.19 in May, 1912. Then followed a long period of accumulation in 1913 and 1914. In June and July, 1914, prices were again down to 84 cents, the last low level of 1911. Here was a period from October, 1912, to July, 1914, when prices held in a range of 6 to 10 cents per bushel most of the time, which plainly showed another period of big accumulation the same as was shown in 1906 and 1907.

The war broke out the latter part of July and the advance started. When prices crossed the accumulation level of $1.00 it plainly indicated a big advance. Despite the fact that this country had a large crop and enormous surplus, prices advanced to 1.32 in September, 1914. Then reacted to 1.11 and after several months of accumulation, advanced to 1.67 in February, 1915, at which level, you can see, they held for about four months while distribution was taking place. Prices declined to 93 cents in September, 1915; advanced to 1.38 in January, 1916; declined to 1.04 in May, 1916.

After this, the scarcity of Wheat in Europe and the enormous buying by foreign countries, carried prices to 3.25 in May, 1917, when the Government stopped trading in Futures and fixed the price of Cash Wheat at $2.50 per bushel. Trading started again in July, 1920. The December option opened at 2.75. Prices continued downward until April, 1921, when the May option reached 1.20. Then followed a squeeze during May, 1921, which carried the May option up to 1.85. In November, 1921, the price again declined to 1.04, which was the last low level reached in May, 1916.

Then followed several months of accumulation in a narrow range, as you can see from the chart, and in February, 1922, May Wheat advanced to 1.49 7/8. You can see that during the months of February, March and April it advanced to around this same level, but failed to exceed the top made in February. During the early days of May, 1922, the May option was selling at 1.47, and everybody was bullish and hoping for $2.00 Wheat, but the chart, which is a record of the tape and shows the balance of supply and demand, plainly indicated that somebody had been supplying Wheat between 1.44 and 1.48 for nearly four months.

The decline in May, 1922, was rapid, carrying prices down to 1.16. Wheat continued to slowly work lower, and the May option declined to 1.05 in August, 1922. It remained between 1.12 and 1.06 during August, September, and October; then crossed this level and advanced to 1.26 3/4 in December, 1922. Note that the last low level, 1.04, was made in May, 1916, and again the same level in November, 1921, and in August, 1922, 1.05, which was practically the same level. The next time that Wheat declines to 1.04 for the May option, it will indicate lower prices and will probably continue down to around 93 cents to 90 cents per bushel. Should it cross the last level, 126 3/4, made in December, 1922, it will then be an indication for higher prices.

Make up a chart on any option of Wheat, Corn, Oats or Barley, and judge it in the same way that I have explained and you will be able to determine the zones of accumulation and distribution. When once prices break out of these zones, you should follow the trend until it changes again. Never trade without a reason. Do not sell because prices are high or buy because they are low. Wait until you see an indication that the trend is plainly indicated; then go with it.

WEEKLY CHART

Wheat and Corn make both sharp and flat tops and bottoms. Chart No. 16 a shows weekly high and low on May Wheat. Note on April 16, 1921, May Wheat declined to 1.19; rallied to around 1.32, holding two weeks in a narrow range; then made a rapid advance to 1.85 at the end of May. This was a straight run-up from a sharp bottom in which only two or three weeks were used for accumulation; then a rapid advance on short covering to a new high level.

Note the weekly chart from October, 1921, to January, 1922. You will see that over 14 weeks of accumulation was plainly shown and that prices never got as low as 1.03 1/2, the level reached on November 5, 1921. The fact that they held for a long time without going lower showed accumulation, but if you waited until you had a plain indication, when prices reached 1.20, which was above the accumulation zone, you would have caught a fast advance which carried prices up 28 cents per bushel in four weeks.

After prices reached 1.49 7/8 on February 27, 1922, notice a sharp decline to 1.30 took place. Prices held for four or five weeks in a narrow range, reaching the lowest level, 128 1/2, around April 1 to 8; then advanced again to 1.49. Here they halted, failing to cross the high price of February and for five weeks distribution was going on, giving you plenty of time to sell out and go short with a stop loss order 2 to 3 cents above the high price made in February and the latter part of April.

After this, a rapid decline followed in May and prices worked slowly lower until the May option reached 1.04 1/2 in August and September, 1922. Here you find another level in a narrow range with five or six weeks of accumulation. During the week ended September 23, prices advanced above the accumulation level and showed that the trend had turned up. They reacted after that, but continued to work higher until they reached 1.26 3/4 in December, 1922, and here is where the daily chart helps us to get out near the top.

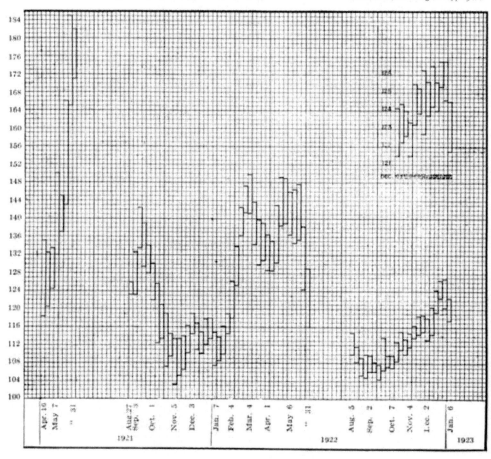

182

DAILY CHART

I have shown on Chart No. 16*b* daily high and low from
December 13 to 29, 1922. Note that on December 20
prices reached 126 1/4; on December 22, 1.26 1/2; on December 27, 1.26 3/4 and on December 28, the high was 1.26 1/2,
from which the decline started. The high price on December
18 was 1.25 1/2 and for ten days prices failed to gain more
than 1 cent per bushel, which showed that a level had been
reached where supply was in excess of demand and after this
period of time when prices broke back below 1.25, which
was under the distribution zone on the daily chart, it was an
indication to sell out and go short. Thus you see that the
daily chart will help to give you a minor change and get you
in or out close to tops and bottoms before the weekly and
monthly charts show a change in the major trend. But the
daily chart will often fool you, as the time period is short
and many false moves occur which are the reverse of the
main trend and do not in any way change it.

DETERMINING CHANGE IN TREND

By study and experience and by considering the activity
of the market, you will often be able to determine very
quickly an important change in trend. Of course, there is
no way of knowing the exact amount of Wheat or Corn
traded in daily; therefore the only way to judge when there
is a large volume of business, is by the rapidity of the fluctuations. For instance:

Suppose May Wheat trades between 1.24 and 1.26 during the day, but fluctuates between the high and low price
five or six times; that is, moving up or down over the same
range. Then we would conclude that there was a large
volume of business being transacted and that somebody was
supplying large quantities of Wheat around 1.26 and buying
around 1.24. Now, if it declines the next day below 1.24,
it would be an indication that support had been withdrawn,
or if it advances above 1.26, it would be an indication that
the supply of Wheat at that level had been absorbed and that
prices are going higher. But suppose the same day Wheat

trades between 1.24 and 1.26, it simply opens at 1.24 and
advances to 1.26 without making any reverse moves up or
down. Then we would conclude that the volume of trading
was not large enough to indicate that it was getting ready
for any immediate change in trend.

SUPPLY AND DEMAND

When a market starts to advance, it continues upward
until it reaches a level where supply and demand are about
equal and prices come to a standstill. Then supply increases
until it exceeds demand, and prices start to decline.

In a long decline or a long advance, a level is reached
where the supply is absorbed and prices go on to the next
level, where they meet another large supply and absorb it,
and finally to a level where the supply is so much greater
than the demand that distribution takes place and prices start
on a long trend down. This is why many weeks and sometimes several months are required at bottom or top to complete accumulation or distribution before a big move starts.

People who buy or sell the first or second time that the
market halts after the trend turns, invariably lose money
because it is simply a halting period to absorb offerings or
to supply a demand at that level, after which the main trend
moves on to the next level. For this reason, it does not pay
to buck the trend -- always go with it. If you trade against
the trend for a quick turn and get a small profit, accept it;
do not expect too much. At the same time, protect your
trade with a stop loss order and do not let it run against you
when you are bucking the trend.

SELECTING A BROKER

Last, but not least of all, selecting a reliable broker is most important. Millions and millions of dollars have been lost during the last few years through failures of unreliable brokers. Therefore, it is just as important to know that your money is safe and that you will get your capital and profits if you make them, as it is to know when to buy and sell.

Make the proper investigation and be sure your broker is safe, not only as to his financial standing, but also try to ascertain whether he or his firm speculates. I do not consider any broker safe who speculates or permits others to speculate on a credit with the firm or customers' money.

I do not advise trading at all with brokers who are not members of the New York Stock Exchange, New York Cotton Exchange, or Chicago Board of Trade. There are a few houses who are members of other exchanges that are honest and reliable. Therefore, investigate the house before you open an account.

I have written what I believe is required for your success. It is practical and based on the result of my years of labor and experience. Read this book over several times, for each time you will learn something new and get new ideas of your own which will benefit you. If you will follow the instructions carefully and trade conservatively, never buying or selling a stock without a reason nor being in too big a hurry to get in or out, I feel sure that you will make a success and after a few years will have cause to thank me for starting you on the right road to Successful Speculation and Investment.

W. D. GANN.

FINIS